Praises for
The Habis of Unity
12 Months to a Stronger An ime

It already makes me feel like I belong. by being a better person.

  – Helen Angel, Homemaker

Your writing style makes me feel like I am a good friend you are talking with. I am inspired.

  – Kathleen Isaacs Ph.D.

I was asked to edit this book for grammar and punctuation and it has already changed my life.

  – Tracy Heinlein, Teacher

I like this whole concept and what I've seen. Like eating potato chips, I might not be able to read just one inspiration each day.

  – Beryle Greenwald, Head Start Pre-school Teacher

A man might think at first that this book is for women but it's NOT. Many people in my business don't listen and aren't patient. I wish they would read this book.

  – Jeff Greenwald, Electrical Engineer

I expected more of a teaching thing and was delighted to find the daily inspirations so interesting and enjoyable - besides being short, to the point and easily remembered.

  – Beverly Deeds, Secretary

I can incorporate the inspirations into my daily life.

  – Patty Sparrow, Resource Manager - Info Systems

I look forward to reading the daily habit reminders to my audience of seniors, who are looking forward to hearing them just as much as me.

  – Bobbi Haskell, Senior Center Aid

It's certainly not dry reading.

  – Barbara Miller, Author, Dearest Max

If people used the Golden Rule more often the world would be better. I can do this because each day is not long - you can read it in a minute.

  – Betsy Fritz, Stock person

I think this would be good for parents to use to teach kids. It's simple to read.

  – Erin Wenzel, Nurse's Aid

The 12 habits are great tools to help people gain the super powers of common sense and common courtesy. They reach more people and positively impact more lives in more places - to become happier and healthier.

  – Karl Ohrman, CLU,
    Coordinated Private Wealth, LLC & Pittsburg Rotary Club

THE HABITS OF UNITY

12 Months to a Stronger America

...one citizen at a time

Together, we uplift ourselves and heal the country we share

ELAINE PARKE, MBA, CS, CM, NSA

Graphic Design by Kurt Griffith

"Together we heal the country we all share."

– Elaine Parke, Author

"We are what we repeatedly do.
Excellence then, is not an art but a habit."

– Aristotle, Classic Greek philosopher

"Civilization is just the slow process of learning to be kind."

– Will and Auriel Durant, Historians

outskirts press

Outskirtspress.com

THE HABITS OF UNITY
12 Months to a Stronger America...One Citizen at a Time
Together, we uplift ourselves and heal the country we share

Requests for information should be directed to All of Us, Inc., at our website: *www.12habits4allofus.org.*

Outskirts Press, Inc.
http://www.outskirtspress.com

ISBN: 978-1-9772-4276-1

Cover Deign © 2021 Elaine Parke & Kurt Griffith.
All rights reserved - Photography liscensed and used with permission.

Outskirts Press and the "OP" logo are trademarks belonging to Outskirts Press, Inc.

Printed in the United States of America

CULTURAL/SOCIAL ISSUES
SELF-HELP

FAMILY & RELATIONSHIPS

Happiness
Motivational
Interpersonal Relations

SEL016000
SEL021000
FAM027000

Library of Congress Catalog Number
LCCN   00-190199

ATTENTION: If you are a non-profit organization or business interested in quantity discounts, or if you simply can't afford the price of this book but would like to have one, please contact us through our website at: *www.12habits4allofus.org.*

Dedication

To YOU.

I wrote this book for you. You and your happier life ahead are the future of my work. You can imagine your photo is in the square below or personalize your book by actually placing your photo or favorite symbol here.

This book is also dedicated to the thousands of treasured youth and family members over the many years, without whose leadership, input and caring creativity, the uplifting and positive changes in schools and communities would never have happened. I am so very grateful.

Specifically, I will always be grateful to my late husband, George O. Parke, who introduced the germ of my idea to the people of Somerset PA where it all started. Also, to our longest enduring board member and contributor, Ralph Moore who has been there for me and the 12 habits work from the very beginning.

Certainly, this dedication must include our first school principal, Dr. Melvin Steals who wrote this book's Forward. Finally, the book is dedicated to Carol York, a loving and talented professional who most helped launch the 12 habits model in Berkeley Springs, WV.

Thank you all, so very much.

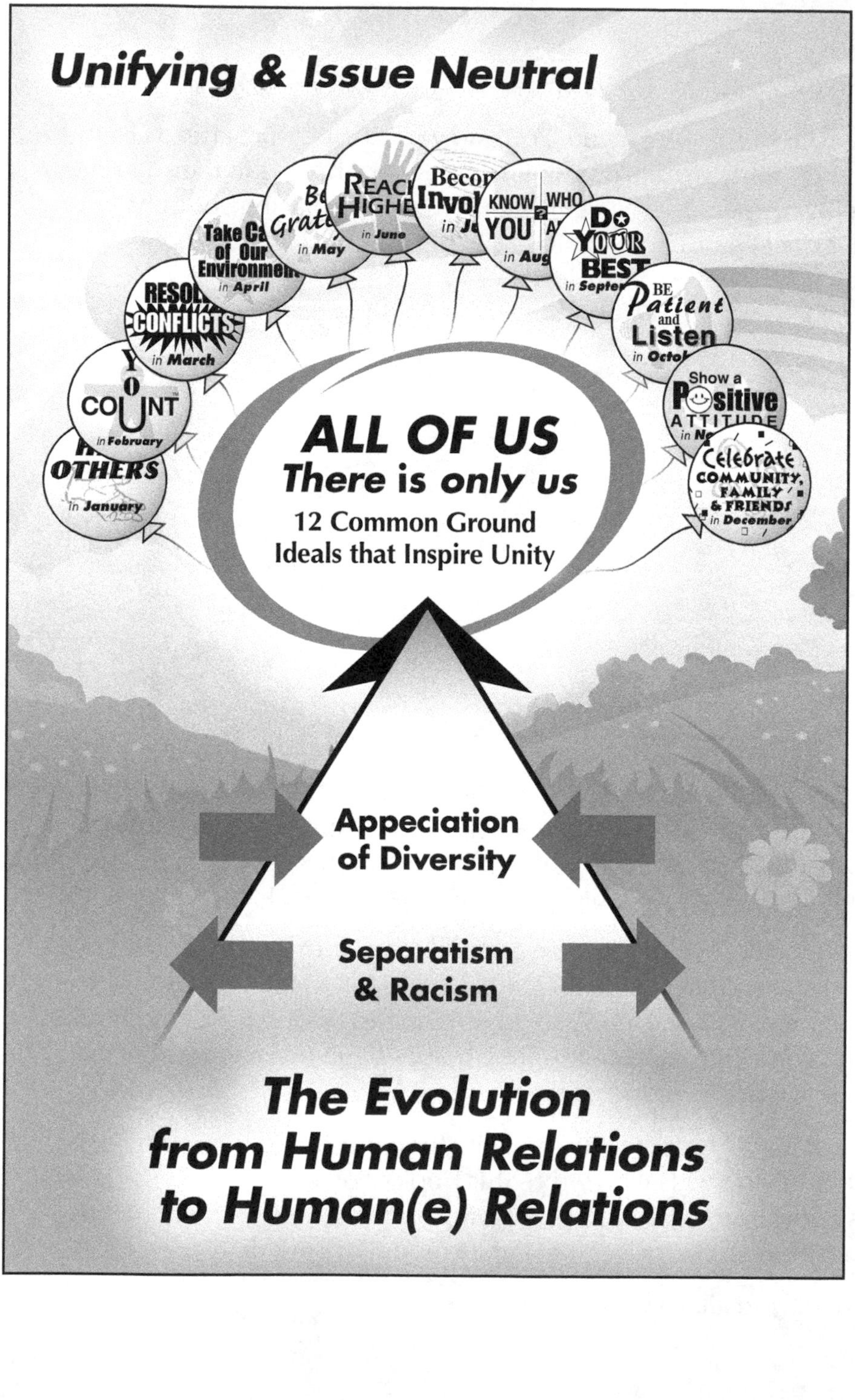
Unifying & Issue Neutral
OTHERS
in January
COUNT
in February
CONFLICTS
in March
Take Ca
of Our
Environmen
in April
in May
REACH
HIGHE
in June
Becom
Invol
KNOW WHO
YOU
in Aug
DO YOUR BEST
BE
Patient
and
Listen
Show a
Positive
Celebrate
COMMUNITY,
FAMILY
& FRIENDS
in December
ALL OF US
There is only us
12 Common Ground
Ideals that Inspire Unity
Appeciation
of Diversity
Separatism
& Racism
The Evolution
from Human Relations
to Human(e) Relations

TABLE OF CONTENTS

THE HABITS OF UNITY
12 Months to a Stronger America...
one citizen at a time
Together, we uplift ourselves and heal the country we share.

365 HABIT-BUILDING MOTIVATIONALS...one month at a time

It's spring! Make a fresh start by resolving conflicts - start at home if need be.

TODAY, I nourish my habit to Take Care of Our Environment
With 30 Environmental Tips
Color - Spring Green
Health Focus – Breathe Deep - Be Smoke FREE!
Happy Earth Month!
Spring's beauty reminds us of nature. Our environment needs us to reduce, reuse and recycle.

TODAY, I cherish my habit to Be Grateful
With 31 "Praise" Phrases"
Color - Grateful Pink
Health Focus – Exercise! Appreciate Your Body.
Happy Mothers' Day!
Stop and smell the flowers. Appreciate all the people and good things in your life.

TODAY, I discover my habit to REACH HIGHER
With 30 "Doing Differently" Tips
Color - JOLT! Orange
Health Focus –Improve Your Health. Start NOW!
Happy Father's Day!
Dream, uplift, and renew. Start a personal betterment project and make a new friend.

TODAY, I honor my habit to Become Involved
With 31 Civic and Volunteer Opportunities
Color - Patriot Red
Health Focus – Fight Viruses by Practicing
Good Hygiene & Cleanliness -
Happy 4th of July!
Remember the dream of our patriot fathers – a UNITED States of America. Celebrate by volunteering to help in your community.

TODAY, I reflect on my habit to Know Who I am
With 31 Fortune Cookie Philosophies
Color - Thoughtful Blue
Health Focus – Health Education and Understanding Vaccines
Happy Summer!
Relax - take a vacation with quiet time to think about what's important to you and your family.

FOREWARD

Melvin H. Steals, PhD
Educator and Grammy Award winning songwriter

Dear Readers of *"The Habits of Unity,"*

Introducing Elaine Parke's "12 monthly habits" into my middle school near Pittsburgh 20 years ago, had a miraculous effect. It not only transformed its dangerous culture into a much safer one, but also increased our students' academic achievement. Moreover, in less than 18 months, our school won a Pennsylvania Department of Health's highly regarded, "Violence Free Youth Challenge Award" as well as a $5,000 check.

Because of the 12 habits, our 8th-grade students entered high school better prepared to learn and less likely to cause classroom disruptions. Our once low-performing district gradually elevated itself off of Pennsylvania's list of 10 worst-performing school districts. I can personally attest to the sterling results that fidelity to Elaine's carefully crafted 12-month process can produce.

Because of that, I have been an avid supporter and a staunch advocate for the 12 habits process for the past 20 years. My wife, Adrena, and I have developed a life-long friendship with Elaine, and together, over the years, we have visited many of her 12 habits communities and schools. During every visit, I feel the uplifting energy and magic her work inspires among the citizens, the staff and the students.

I am not only a professional educator, but also have contributed to our music culture, co-writing many songs with my twin brother – most well-known of which is "Could it Be I'm Falling In Love." Like music, Elaine's 12 Habits make harmony out of discord among people wherever it goes.

Junior High School Students carrying 12 Habits Banners in Apple Butter Festival Parade in Berkeley Springs, WV.

Some of the Awards earned and presented to the *12 Habits 4 All of Us* campaign over the years, including the London Institute for Social Invention's designation as a Social Invention.

QUICK START INSTRUCTIONS

With 12 Mental Health Habits – we will uplift ourselves and heal the country we share.

SPECIAL NOTE: This book and these 12 MENTAL HEALTH HABITS are for EVERYONE, EQUALLY. The most important statement I want to make in this entire book - is that every single person is valued, honored and respected for who they are. Welcome to BECOMING UNITY IN AMERICA. I'm very glad you're here.

– Elaine Parke, MBA, CS, CM, NSA

With this book, you have in your hand a do-it-yourself path to better mental health. It is a "one-minute a day," magical guide to a better life and more empowered citizenship. Each of the 12 months of the year is branded with one colorful habit-forming mental health theme like resolve conflicts, help others, and be more positive.

Please note: This book contains a pro-active mental health protocol that is not a substitute for professional mental health therapy and counseling. If you are in therapy or in need of therapy, using this book will help you do a better job of responding to the therapeutic counseling available to you. It is not a substitute for therapy but will work hand-in-hand with therapy to improve your ability to lead a happier and more fulfilling life.

There are hundreds of published books about habits, but none of them build good habits FOR you and WITH you. With less than one quick and energizing minute a day, this book will do just that. These Mental Health Habits will give you a better life and will also inspire you as a better citizen.

There are several introductory and closing chapters all about my history and how this 12-month protocol works and why, if you are interested. However, you don't need to read them right now unless you prefer to know more before beginning your own good habits adventure.

Instead, you can just get started by going straight to the 365 Daily Motivational Readings section and find today's date. Begin your one-minute a day, all-new improved life on whatever day this is for you right now. Like brushing your teeth, it's so easy to keep your one-magic-minute a day good habit going day after day, month by month, and year after year.

Like holidays, this habit-forming pattern isn't meant to end – ever. Just return each year to revitalize and renourish your commitment to each month's mental health value. This is a gift you give to yourself and it is absolutely FREE! Time is the greatest equalizer. Everyone has the same 1,440 minutes to spend every day. We can each choose to make life better for ourselves and others – or not. Certainly, we have a happier life when we do.

I wrote this book because, like me, you may find it stressful to feel like a helpless bystander in this toxic era of division in America. If you really think about it however, national unity won't trickle down to help us. Good citizens like us must trickle up, and add "our better selves" to the progress toward more unity that we all dream of. Tim Shriver said it very well in his 2020 book, *The Call to Unite.*

"Uniters do not expect uniformity of opinion, but do seek unity in treating others with dignity – which gives justice a chance to flourish."

With this book, you and other readers have a personal tool for staying focused on what we do have power over; the choices we make with our own daily attitudes and actions. You will find that the 365 one-minute readings are grouped to focus on forming one habit per month. Think of them as 12 "New Month's" resolutions instead of 1 New Year's resolution.

Taken all together, these 12 habits motivate us to improve ourselves and our relationships, AND, to value the earth we all share. Each day's reading has a little different perspective and an "action" tip. Each month, the readings have a different "personality." For instance, I tell little jokes in November to inspire a positive attitude. There are daily suggestions for helping others in January.

As an MBA and former advertising professional whose personal passion is to help people get along better, I came up with this 12 month, "one-habit-a-month" game plan. I've been waging this crusade to inspire "getting along better," in schools and communities for 30 years. In the community/school format, the 12 habits are promoted in the community climate, much like holidays; with radio,

TV, posters, flyers, and group events, celebrations, and activities.

The momentum of this mission reached several million people in Pittsburgh and surrounding Pennsylvania communities and results were evaluated by nine independent studies. It was named a Social Invention by the London Institute for Social Inventions.

Overall, 72% of surveyed citizens said they felt more connected to others. 37% said they'd improved their behaviors. Student conflicts in schools were reduced by up to 62% in less than two years and academics improved. One surveyed student said, *"I'm now nice to the people I used to be mean to. This is COOL. I might even get better grades too"*

I have been proving the ability of these 12 action habits to uplift and unify people for 30 years and now this book will reach many more Americans like you. More than a book, it's a mission to heal America one citizen at a time - and it needs help from readers all across our great country.

Starting right now, today, we can build the momentum towards more equality and unity in America while uplifting our own lives too. This is the win-win cliché of all time – together we don't fall down, we all lift up.

Even though the daily book motivationals will help you form better habits, you can get creative and expand the ways you re-mind yourself. For instance, my own closet looks like a thrift store rack because my clothes are arranged by the colors on the front of this book. I really do wear "the color-of-the-month" as an extra reminder.

I love doing it really. I have found over the years that it's an easy way to actually wear more of the clothes I have. I'm pleased when an old favorite skirt or blouse shows up to wear again as I color-coordinate with each month, year after year. The creative possibilities are endless.

You may want to use the unity habits and quotes and little jokes from the book to make your social media posts more interesting. You can carry out your own "unity" mission in other ways to "pay it forward" to your family and friends. If we haven't learned much else from social media, we've learned that shared thoughts, whether they are good or bad, or truth or fake; become powerful beyond measure when they reach lots of people at the same time and are repeated over and over again.

Remember, This isn't a book ABOUT habits – it is a HABIT-FORM-ING book. When many other readers, like you, take it home and begin their "one-minute-a day" habit building adventure, their lives and outlooks will brighten and so will the climate of relationships that define this, our democratic citizenship.

"Now more than ever, America needs this unifying year-round mental health plan, deemed a social invention by the London Institute, and already proven successful by, Elaine Parke, a social transformation visionary."

> – Melvin H Steals PhD
> Educator and Grammy Award winning songwriter

12 HABITS AS A MONTHLY REMINDER SYSTEM....

Month after month, year after year.... until we all celebrate the joy of comm-unity as never before.

"Excellence is an art won by training and habituation. We do not act rightly because we have virtue but we rather have virtue because we have acted rightly.

We are what we repeatedly do. Excellence then, is not an art, but a habit."
  – Aristotle

NOTE: Remember, this book is habit-forming and may cause a happier life. Even though the book's annual sequence begins with JANUARY and ends with DECEMBER, you do NOT have to start in January. You can START RIGHT NOW!! Just find the current month and the day and BEGIN. Each month is introduced with some inspiration and a motivational goal to get you started.

The essence of this book is this. You can spend lots of time and money buying and reading self-help books and blogs, watching podcasts and seminars, going to conferences and seeking the next best wisdom and advice all your life. However, if you don't incorporate that help and advice into the habitual daily practices in your own life, you've wasted your time and money.

Speak with care,
Your words become actions,

Act with care,
Your actions become habits

Repeat an act with care,
Your habits become character.

Form your character with care,
Your character becomes your destiny.
  – Jim Ryun, SEEN ON THE WALL AT SIR SPEEDY PRINTING COMPANY

There is great power in establishing healthy mental routines for ourselves. If you think about it the way we think about our bodies, consuming healthy "mind-minutes" is good nutrition for our souls. It is certainly as important as consuming vitamin-enriched calories is to our bodies. What's most exciting is that each of us can empower ourselves with just a few minutes a day, to make our own lives better and the lives of those around us.

There is a whole new concept being introduced here that might be called "Mental Nutrition." We all know that to advertisers, for instance, we are called "consumers." To them, we are potential consumers for their advertised products and services. We are also consumers of food and we make a big fuss over recipes and cooking and of course, about diets for when we 'consume" too much food or too many calories that are not nutritious.

Here, I've introduced the concept of "mind-minutes" or "mental consumption" which is that we "consume" information or messages and that, just like food, what our minds are consuming, may or may not, be good for our mental health. Occasionally we read about restricting how many hours kids use electronics, but to date, we haven't taken the idea of the quality of our "mental consumption" of messages as seriously as we do our financial expenditures or calorie consumption.

This book contains a unifying year-round plan to practice together the needed art of getting along better with one another by engaging a system of healthy mental health habit-building messaging. It uses the months and colors as reminders to build good habits we all can celebrate and follow, all together at the same time.

Colors are awesome as additional cues for remembering to practice these 12 mental health habits. In communities where these habits are practiced, they use the 12 "caring-colors" as additional reminders. Each color has its own special name that fits the habit of the month, like "Slow-down Lavender" for being patient in October.

The names of the months are to the 12 unity habits, what brand names are to the products we buy, like Nike, or Apple or Coke. The names of the months and the colors are unique" cues" to help us remember the mental health habits they signify.

Sometime during the 30 years of our "12 Habits" activities in communities and schools, we also developed a physical "Health Focus" that is uniquely suited to the social theme of each month. In this book we share the health focuses with you but they are not part of the habit-forming mind-minutes in this book. It is likely that it will take another whole book to put the health habits into a habit-forming pattern for you. Meanwhile, you can get started practicing the health habits on your own.

To close out this section on using the 12 months as a reminder system, I looked on the internet for testimonials about habit-building. I found that many, many famous people have commented on the subject of habit-building, as far back as Aristotle and Confucius. Here's a few of these testimonial quotes for you to consider as you begin your own habit-forming journey here.

There is great power in living a routine built from habit-forming. Brushing your teeth daily helps keep your teeth from falling out for instance. Don't worry, there's plenty of room in your days for off-plan adventures and excitement; likely even more, when you've got the basics of your life in hand and under control.

People's natures are alike; it is their habits that separate them.
— **Confucius, Chinese Sage and Politician**

We are what we repeatedly do. Excellence then, is not an act but a habit.
— **Aristotle, Classic Greek philosopher**

The successful person makes a habit of doing what the failing person doesn't like to do.
— **Thomas Edison, American Inventor of the Electric Light Bulb**

There is no elevator to success, you have to take the stairs.
— **Zig Ziglar, One of America's Most Famous "Encouragers"**

Feeling sorry for yourself and your present condition is not only a waste of energy but the worst habit you could possibly have.
— **Dale Carnegie, Motivational Success Trainer and Author**

Our character is basically a composite of our habits. Because they are consistent, often unconscious patterns, they constantly, daily, express our character.

   – Stephen Covey

The good habits you cultivate put your dreams within your reach.

   – Elaine Parke

Discipline is choosing between what you want now and what you want most.

   – Abraham Lincoln, 16th President of the United States

In essence, if we want to direct our lives, we must take control of our consistent actions. It's not what we do that shapes our lives, but what we do consistently.

   – Tony Robbins

Habit is a cable; we weave a thread each day.

   – Horace Mann, American Educational Reformer

12 HABITS FROM A
NATIONAL UNITY PERSPECTIVE

> *O, let America be America again – The land that never has been yet – And yet must be – the land where every man is free.*
> **– Langston Hughes, Great American Poet**

National unity will never trickle down. More good citizens who are free, but also responsible citizens, must trickle up. If we are to unite an authentic democracy – a community of equality in America, it must be each of us, one citizen at a time, who, with our own responsible actions, treat ourselves and others with dignity while we move through our own days.

I have an audacious perspective, that our forefathers are effectively to blame for the 245 years of "self-rights driven strife" that we Americans suffer from. They screwed up because they wrote a Bill of Rights but failed to write a Bill of Responsibilities.

It's understandable. They were rebels against the tyranny of the English Crown. Entombing our rights was paramount. Now, with democracy circling the drain, while nearly every American has their own, "I deserve my rights platform," we've jumped from a melting pot into a stewing pot.

> *"Uniters do not expect uniformity of opinion, but do seek unity in treating others with dignity – which gives justice a chance to flourish."*
> **– Tim Shriver, Editor of** *The Call to Unite:*
> *Voices of Hope and Awakening.* **(2021)**

There is no need to abandon the beauty of America as a land of individualism and rights. However, as citizens of a democracy, beyond voting and obeying the laws, we are also obliged to treat one another with dignity, make an effort to be our "best selves" in our own lives, and to cherish our children and our earth. These are simple responsibilities we all can agree on, but sometimes life gets away from us, and we forget these things in the heat of life's complexities.

What we need is to balance our American right to have rights, by acting responsibly as citizens, so that we maintain the integrity of the core of democracy – and that is us. We not only must be "of and for the people," but also "by" the people, acting in cooperation as dignified citizens whenever we can.

Simple ideals that support treating ourselves, each other, and our earth with dignity are the basis for the 12 habits in this book and I propose, are the basis for a "Bill of Responsibilities" that will make us all - both happier and better citizens.

My work of the last many years has pioneered a unique broad-reach initiative to inspire improved human relations in families, schools and communities; perhaps more than ever before. The pay it forward, ripple effect of the 12 habits monthly model has already proven, among several million in the greater Pittsburgh region, that we can all learn basic social skills and democratic ideals together. Independent community surveys reported that in less than two years, 72% felt more connected to one another and 37% improved their actions – at least once.

Together, when we share the observance of one colorful ideal, one month at a time, just like we observe holidays, we create a ripple effect. As the ripples expand, they will improve the inter-personal "climate" in our country and makes it easier for those with differences, to seek common ground. Together we will change the momentum away from division and towards effectively addressing and solving our issues.

Practicing the 12 values in this book is one way you become part of this expanding ripple of unity in America. You are empowered and powerful. This is just NOT difficult. These values are simple codes of daily life that too often get lost in the morass of negativity. Unconstrained information, overwhelmingly streams around us on television and throughout the social media internet.

When more people are celebrating these 12 habits, with their own actions and creativity, the months of the year will become building blocks towards a mentally healthier climate in families and neighborhoods, and in schools and communities and eventually, all across America.

Just like we celebrate holidays together, we will all together know which colorful unity habit to celebrate each month and the ripple momentum will grow. Holidays unite us because we all know when to celebrate them all together. They inspire our creativity and collective regard for our common good. I believe that the challenges to our earth's climate will not be effectively addressed until our person-to-person climate of human relationships is healed.

Our very existence simply cannot afford the costs of excessive strife and conflict among us when we have common challenges that only a unified effort has any hope of overcoming. Human nature MUST evolve to become "humane" nature. We've known all along that the Golden Rule is the standard for getting along together but for thousands of years we just haven't done it very well.

We have committed the Golden Rule to memory;
let us now commit it to life.
— **Edwin Markham, American Poet, Man With the Hoe**

By breaking the essence of the Golden Rule down into 12 specific actions, one month at a time, that uplift and unify us, like "Be Patient & Listen" in October, we are each reminded to support our societal role as citizens of a democracy. Our country needs all of us to participate by listening, understanding, negotiating, and cooperating with one another as much as possible.

"And so, my fellow Americans: ask not what your country can
do for you—ask what you can do for your country."
— **John F. Kennedy, 35th President of the United States**

President Kennedy framed the "participative citizens" attitude towards our country that we often quote but rarely make the focus of our "call to action" to American citizens. Perhaps, had he lived out his Presidency, he would have called for a citizens "Bill of Responsibilities" to be enacted.

What we have now are these 12 actions as useful habit-forming tools for taking personal responsibility for getting along with one another, for living more meaningful lives, and for being as self-sufficient as possible in a democratic nation. This is about sharing the practical Golden Rule truth that is both common sense and common among all belief systems. This book is intended to be a 21st century version of Thomas Paine's book of "Common Sense."

As you share these 12 habits adventures with me, you are joining many other people who are celebrating life and becoming a stronger America, by practicing the monthly habits at the same time as you are. Everyone, individually, creates their own observances and celebrations in their homes, communities, schools, work places and in their interest groups and/or places of worship. No two families celebrate Thanksgiving exactly the same way, even though they are sharing a common observance to be thankful for all that we have.

Remember, this is a book about a new - year-round plan to reach out and join us together to improve our personal lives, our shared experiences and our own personal power to unify America. These pages are your HANDBOOK and your own personal "daily reminder system" to help you convert the Golden Rule into a more enriched and fulfilled life. The 12 months become our shared building blocks towards a new mental health culture in America.

It is my vision, that in addition to readers across America practicing their one-minute a day habit-building; the local and national media will also join in to help spread the monthly messages through mass media and social media, like "pay it forward." The outcome will be an improved inter-personal "climate" in America where the work of skilled mental health experts will have a better chance at healing the lives of those they work with.

Nationally we have engaged mass media advertising for good before. It is called "Cause Marketing." Now is the time to do it again on behalf of reducing stressful division and for healing ourselves and our country. American citizens have responded to cause advertising campaigns to "Buckle UP" and "Don't Drink and Drive." More recently we've seen and responded to ad campaigns for "Love Has No Labels" and "Wear Masks and Social Distance."

The point I'm making is drawn from an old Cherokee parable and it is one of my life's favorites. It is called *"The Wolf You Feed."*

One evening, an old Cherokee grandfather is telling his grandson about a battle between two wolves that is going on inside all of us.

My son, he says "There is a good wolf of joy, peace, love, hope, serenity, humility, kindness, benevolence, empathy, generosity, truth, compassion and faith.

There is also a bad wolf of anger, envy, regret, greed, arrogance, self-pity, guilt, resentment, false pride, superiority and ego."

The grandson thought about his grandfather's words for a few moments and then asked, *"WHICH WOLF WINS?"*

The old Cherokee, with a twinkle in his eye, replied simply, "THE WOLF YOU FEED."

The techno-consumerism and politically motivated divided climate we live in and whose messages we consume, has its foot on the scale favoring the bad wolf. This is why it is our own responsibility to consume messages that build the qualities of the good wolf in us, as many religions and ethicists try to do. This book contains 365 days of good wolf messages presented in a way that can help shape our habits for the future.

When reading each magic one-minute a day "habit" action for yourself, you are choosing to build habits that will help heal yourself and America by repeating, reinforcing, and practicing the specific mental health actions and make them habits for you. You are empowering yourself to be in charge of your own good choices.

If you've noticed, I've sometimes repeated my important ideas in this book because what the techno-advertisers know is that it is repetition that helps us remember and act. That's the secret to what impels us to buy insurance from lizards and drink 35 billion dollars' worth of a sticky brown sweet liquid branded by the name, "COKE."

If you're really motivated to feed your good wolf, you can do more than just read the one-minute action reminders. Personally, I "wear" the color of the month most days as my fashion statement. I make monthly habit reminder sticky notes for each area of my office and home where I spend a lot of my time. Of course, most of all, I share the monthly habits on my social media sites and I hope you will share them too.

There is destiny that makes us brothers:
None goes his way alone:
All that we send into the lives of others
Comes back onto our own.

I care not what his temples or his creeds,
One thing holds firm and fast

That into his fateful heap of days and deeds
The soul of man is cast.
   — **Edwin Markham, American Poet, Man With the Hoe**

The monthly celebration of these habits is the way we can all come together at the same time in mutually beneficial common thought and practices. The 12 months, as habit-forming blocks of time, become the building blocks for a new mental health culture in America.

These pages are your HANDBOOK and your own personal "daily reminder system" to help you convert the habits of common sense living into a more enriched and fulfilled life. Remember, "This book is habit-forming and may cause a happier life."

Civilization is just the slow process of learning to be kind.
   — **Will and Ariel Durant, *The Lessons of History***

A local family making 12 Unity Habits Posters at the County Fair in Morgan County, WV - then called 12 Habits of Wonderful People because of the Wild and Wonderful West Virginia slogan.

A LITTLE HISTORY

Perhaps you are interested in knowing how the UNITY HABITS came about and why each month was chosen to celebrate that habit.

It all began in 1987 when I became inspired with the idea that each month of the year could be designated as a "branded" period of time to celebrate one aspect of good mental health living. It takes 21-30 days to form a habit so one month is the perfect length of time.

A few years later, I became Director of Marketing for a resort near a small town of about eleven thousand people in south western Pennsylvania. This community was the first town that got together and tried out this infant idea. You'll read more details in the "30 Years of Making the 12 Habits COOL" section of the book.

A group of community citizens became interested and met together every month to work on how the 12 months of action habits plan would work. The group included the Mayor, the Chief of Police, the Director of the County Welfare Office, the Chairman of the Ministerial Association, the Superintendent of Schools, the Executive Director of the local Chamber of Commerce, the owner of a local printing company, the owner of the local radio station, and students from the local high school, plus other residents, neighbors, volunteers and friends.

For nearly a year they met to compose the 12 Habits and select which month to celebrate each habit. Then, we formed a non-profit called, All of Us, Inc., that still exists today and manages the community/school initiatives. The Unity Habits in this book are the outcomes of the spirit and dedication of a group of people who volunteered their time to help give birth to the 12 Unity Habits mental health plan.

The collaboration was a pure community endeavor - reflecting the perspective of everyone. For me, every day will always be a "Be Grateful" day when I think of this committed group who lent their

The author displaying the Rwandan version of the 12 Habits logo. A delegation from Rwanda attended a Rotary International comference in 2005, looking for a project to inspire their youth to maintain peaceful relationships with one another. They wanted to forever avoid another genocide episode. They were taking the habit to "Resolve Conflicts" to a National Level.

spirits, their minds and their hearts to build the foundation of what you have in your hand today. Thank you, everyone.

Step back for a minute and look, with me, at the big picture. If we all start practicing these unifying and uplifting habits every day, every month, and all month long, our lives will become uplifted too. Together we will support national mental health and better unify America. The unity habits will strengthen and grow because, just like holidays, we will all be creating and sharing the same monthly action experiences at the same time.

AUTHOR'S BLOG - My Story Behind this Book

Whatever you can do, or dream you can, begin it.
Boldness has genius, power, and magic in it.
— Johann Wolfgang von Goethe

In the simmering hot summer of 1970, I moved to Cleveland, Ohio. Bombarded daily with the heartbreaking news of a student protester shooting at nearby Kent State University, a hole began boring itself into my soul. The profound pain of the nearby suffering in Kent resonated deep among the losses ever simmering within my own heart.

As an ADD hyperactive child, I had too often irritated my mother to the point of abusive explosion. Yet, I naively grew to adulthood without ever understanding why people could treat one another so badly, or why it had happened, so often, to me.

Resiliantly conquering my childhood wounds, and with a talent for writing, I had gone on to build an impressive career in corporate marketing and advertising. The heavy pain of the nearby suffering at Kent continued to resonate discordantly within my own heart. And now, I was sidelined with a newborn and toddler sons. I hugged my babies and settled into my motherhood life in a strange city with no family living nearby.

As the months wore on, I cared for my sons while the pain of loss became more current. With my full support, my husband had graduated from Harvard Business School. Now, his new "fast-track" job kept him away from home almost all of the time. Before Harvard our marriage was splendid -- we were partners in life and love. Now, both the bountiful joys, and also the difficult burdens of parenting, fell on my shoulders.

With my husband rarely at home, there was no one to share the experience. I felt alone and abandoned. He had a "blue chip" career ticket with a Harvard MBA and could have any job he wanted. With a beautiful young family, I couldn't understand why he chose to work so many long hours so far away from his wife and adorable sons who needed him so badly. Was the ambitious pursuit of power and money really worth missing out on the precious joys we already had in our little family and home?

Although I knew that raising my children was the most important job I would ever have, I needed to do something more to fill the growing void inside. I found a church that took care of children for parents who volunteered. Soon, I found myself at Mary B. Martin Elementary School, in the Hough neighborhood of Cleveland, working in Mrs. Porter's first grade classroom.

I was assigned to work with one little girl, Veronda. The school year was nearly over and Veronda hadn't learned her letters and numbers. She was in peril of failing. Veronda and I sat at a special table with learning exercise materials in hand. I wanted her to succeed, but she wasn't interested or paying attention.

Then one morning everything changed for Veronda and for me. Suddenly, the door of the classroom crashed open, as if imploded by a hurricane wind. In stumbled a huge angry but unsteady man, who lunged straight across the room toward Veronda, (and me) with fire in his eyes. I couldn't believe the courage of Mrs. Porter who, with no thought for her own safety, quickly stepped into his path. Miraculously, the man stopped.

By now it was obvious that he was Veronda's father. I watched the fire in his eyes cool, as every child in the room understood he had been dissuaded from taking a next step that might have harmed Veronda. Clearly the rage in their home was spilling over with a momentum of its own, surpassing the man's dim grasp of how to treat the daughter he loved. I looked at Veronda. The cowering fear and vivid pain in her eyes told me her truth.

And it reminded me of mine. I was transformed into that once small girl, cowering in the kitchen corner of my childhood home in Schenectady N.Y. It had felt like being at the bottom of a huge mixing bowl with the cabinets and appliances looming over and around me, trapping me in their space. I was alone with fear, as my mother's rage erupted. She grabbed the paddle from above the refrigerator and rapidly the hail of slaps and blows tumbled down upon me. In memory, I had stepped on the land mine again and awakened the unfulfilled need to be loved inside me. I could relate to Veronda.

When I next returned to Mrs. Porter's classroom and to Veronda, I had a plan. As we moved together toward our work table, I took her hand. Then we sat down to our exercises. But this time, I gently placed one arm across her shoulders, leaving the other arm and hand free to work with the materials. I intuited that even more than learning her letters and numbers, Veronda needed the kind warmth of connection to someone who cared about her and would not hurt her.

Over the next few sessions, I felt Veronda's rigidly fragile little body begin to relax. The attention she had riveted on me, in her need for human connection, was now freed up. She began, for the first time, to pay attention to the exercises. Within two weeks, she completed learning all her letters and numbers and was beginning to recognize and read a few simple words. Although her reading skills were still sub-par, Mrs. Porter felt that she would be able to catch up, and Veronda was passed to the second grade.

Like millions of caring workers and volunteers across America, I had been instrumental in helping one beautiful child inch towards the possibility that her life could become more empowered and successful. However, I was left with the nagging question about the perpetual disparity between resources and need. It is a "bottomless pit" struggle that, when waged one person at a time, is likely to never be won.

I asked the question, "How can we exponentially multiply the helping resources necessary to heal and nourish one another in order to meet the vast needs that abound?" It would be another twenty years before the answer came.

As for me, my marriage didn't survive the four+ years of nearly complete separation. And finding the source of my own demons didn't prevent the tumultuous years that followed. I had hoped that the divorce would motivate my children's father to be at least a part-time parent, but instead he permanently moved far away soon after. I parented the best I could. I took every opportunity to facilitate getting the boys together with their father as often as possible.

In the late 1970's my sons and I became part of the cast of a magical traveling peace play, "Alice in Blunderland" written by two brothers from Kent State, Tim and Tom DeFrange. It was about the, then, nuclear armament build-up between the USA and Russia. We performed in the Canon Caucus Room in the Capitol Complex and at the 1980 Zero Freeze Conference in Washington, D.C. – as well as in communities throughout the northeast.

During this unique experience I saw and felt first-hand, that the

"peace" movement was as disparate and fractious as any other assort-
ment of "almost" like-minded people. The conflicts between groups
was almost ludicrous. I vowed to find a way to bring people together
in peace and unity in an all new and improved, kinder, and more
caring way.

In October of 1987, just before my youngest son left for college, a
powerful vision came to me in the night. It took form as a plan to
fulfill that life dream to inspire more kindness and unity between
people. It burst alive as a brilliant light in my head and heart.

Having had to parent and to work to support my children simultaneously, I had grown professionally to become an executive expert at
marketing and advertising, I had nationally promoted many products
and brand names, from hair spray to weekend vacations. With a small,
creative staff of 12 or more, I had routinely influenced and motivated
the buying behaviors of millions of people.

The vision presented the question, "Why not use your professional
knowledge to develop a strategic year-round plan; one that would
convert each month of the year into a symbol or brand name for one
of 12 aspects of peaceful and unifying actions for living together?
Why not? We've already branded February as Black History Month."

Why couldn't each month become a symbol for one habit-forming
period of time to focus on one aspect of unity and simple mental
health values for getting along better? All across America and in
every country and language around the world we already share the
months in our own languages, but in common. We can create a national and global pattern of celebrating monthly shared and unifying
values that, like reoccuring holidays, can nourish, unify and uplift us
all, year after year.

As the ethereal question burned its way into my spirit and brain, I in-
stinctively withdrew from the awesome burden that I knew was now
upon me. Who was I to think I could build even this worthy vision to
its potential to become a paradigm changing influence of national
and even international influence? Would March's value, to "Resolve
Conflicts," someday become International Resolve Conflicts Month?

My youngest son left for college in 1988. I then moved from Ohio to
the small town of Somerset, PA, where I became the Marketing Director for Hidden Valley Resort. In the first few years of making personal

and professional friendships, I often spoke of the vision I had for making each month of the calendar year a symbol for one of the 12 aspects of "getting along better" living. Then in late 1989, the founder of Hidden Valley, George O. Parke, called a meeting of Somerset's youth and leaders to hear about my vision for unifying and uplifting their schools and their community.

From that moment on, this was no longer my story, but the story of the next 30 years of making the 12 monthly habits prove to be effective and COOL! The story stretches throughout western Pennsylvania including Pittsburgh, and, through Rotary International, into the post genocide African country of Rwanda as a youth peacemaking initiative. This part of the story is in a separate chapter, "30 Years of Making the 12 Habits in Action COOL." Now, 30+ years later, I am still on that path with you, my citizen readers of "The Habits of Unity," here beside me.

Rebuilding who I was as an adult was a trial and error process, with too many marriages and mistakes of my own making. Each moment that I learned and grew, however, I knew that someday, my sons would be able to take responsibility for their own lives. Then I would dedicate the rest of my own life to helping other kids find peace and kindness at home; a home that Veronda and I didn't have and that without their father's presence, I was not able to give to my own sons.

On Rotary International peacekeeping mission in 2006, author, Elaine Parke, was honored to be invited to place flowers on one of the five crypts of the dead at the Kigali National Genocide Memorial. The memorial is the final resting place for more than 259,000 victims of the 1994 genocide.

30 YEARS OF MAKING 12 HABITS IN ACTION "COOL!"

The Story of the Practice of 12 Unity Habits in Communities in America's Midwest

Project organizer Elaine Parke speaks to the audience about the "12 Habits of Wonderful People — Berkeley Springs" project as team member Dana Ryce looks on Thursday evening at The Country Inn of Berkeley Springs.

A nonprofit, tentatively titled "12 Habits of Wonderful People – Berkeley Springs," was formally unveiled Thursday evening during a presentation held at the Country Inn of Berkeley Springs as reported in the Matrinburg Journal. – May 15, 2015..

For nearly 30 years, I've been stewarding a 12 Habits community/ school mental health movement as a "Pay it Forward" kind of plan to unify America by inspiring all of us to uplift our own lives and relationships. The non-profit is All of Us, Inc., and in communities and schools in the Midwest, the initiative was first called, "All of Us, and then became known as "The Caring Habit of the Month Adventure."

In recent years, in West Virginia, it was once again renamed, "The 12 Habits of Wonderful People." Now, although, the focus themes of the 12 action habits have stood the test of time and remained essentially unchanged and unswervingly effective, the name going forward is, "12 Habits 4 All of Us," with information available at the website www.12habits4allofus.org.

These 12 habits to encourage "getting along better" actions and attitudes are essentially based on the most fundamental mental health phrase I know of – the Golden Rule – do to others as you'd like done to you. We've known this for millennia but as a civilization, we haven't seemed capable of making this the primary theme of human relations. That's why I decided that making the Golden Rule COOL, and colorful and fun, and something that everyone is doing – would be a good idea.

Here, I'll share some of the history and wonderful stories of the 12 habits initiatives in so many schools and communities and the fabulous creativity and ingenuity of thousands of people who participated over the years. For me, it has been a journey of love and wonder that certainly hasn't ended yet.

The local community/school plan engages print and electronic media to motivate 12 Monthly Mental Health Habits - or more simply, to inspire and reinforce the family Golden Rule values we all know and love. This includes posters, flyers, radio, TV, print, events, celebrations and social media, all focused on the same value, signified by the same color, for one month.

The 12 habits initiative grew throughout western Pennsylvania because KDKA-TV-CBS in Pittsburgh produced 30-second public service TV ads, for each of the monthly habits and they ran for nearly three years. One local funder, Highmark Blue Cross Blue Shield brought me in to initiate the 12 habits in one school that was violent and poor performing by state standards.

In that school, and in its surrounding community, as in all of the participants thereafter, a local "team" of people was formed who arranged for all the monthly promotional materials to be produced and distributed. The materials were posters, flyers, rack cards, pencils, table tents, wrist bands, and banners, each color-coordinated for the month's habit. Just before the first day of each month, members of the team collected the prior month's materials and distributed the materials for the next month. From there, students and residents became inspired to work the habits into

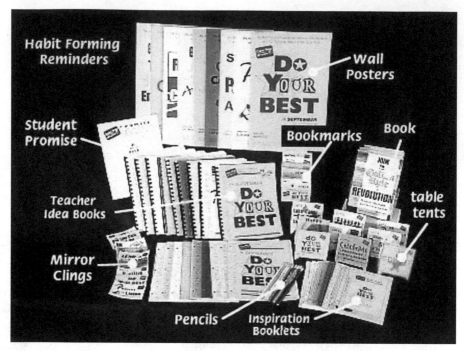

12 Unity Habits materials used for involved communities and schools over the years. Coordinated media scripts for radio, TV and social media are not shown. Each month is printed on the appropriate colors, shown on the cover of this book.

every conceivable area of school/family/community life.

Over the years, the 12 habits movement has positively inspired several million citizens in western Pennsylvania, the eastern panhandle of West Virginia, and was sponsored by Rotary International in post-genocide Rwanda. Community surveys showed that in less than two years in a 12 habits community-building climate, 72% of the citizens felt more "connected" and 39% reported they had acted with more civility at least once.

I wrote this book because as readership grows across the county, the book becomes "media" for the year-round 12 mental health habits plan. As readership grows, the movement towards unity will grow. This book contains short motivationals for every day, that focus on the 12 values. I hope that soon, March will become National Resolve Conflicts month just like February is Black History month. Every month, every American will have a theme to inspire their own actions and creativity to bring it alive in their own lives, and also to motivate their own friends and neighbors.

The Habits of Unity

First, from all of the research over 30 years, I want to share my most favorite quote from one survey of middle schoolers. One student wrote that because he/she repeatedly saw and heard the 12 Habits all over town and was taught them in school, *"I am now nice to the people I used to be mean to. This is cool. I might even get better grades too."*

Motivating even a few more of us to be nice to the people we used to be mean to would go a long way toward unifying and healing America. The divisiveness, racism, and hate in our nation is too often based on each of us blaming someone or something else for all of the problems. To attract audiences with sensationalism, news media tends to exploit stories of our differences rather than focus on stories of the good human qualities we all have in common.

It is a dream I have already proven possible, that the media can someday soon, become a powerful force for GOOD. I'm a former advertising professional and I know the secret of media's power lies in its' repetitiousness and the fact that it reinforces our desires to fill our needs. The repetition makes it easy for us to remember what advertisers want us to do – like NIKE says, "Just Do It!" – meaning buy NIKE shoes. Advertisers and their media are relentlessly repetitious in promoting their brands.

That's why I asked and then answered the question, "How can we use the same repetitious techniques and be relentless about nourishing ourselves to practice good mental health habits?" In that moment of lightning-bolt understanding I had back in 1987, what came to me is the idea that the names of each of the 12 months could be branded with one of 12 good values.

After 25 years as a marketing/ad professional I had taken for granted that, like NIKE, throughout my career I had engaged mass-media to guide the buying habits of my consumers. Marketing is a sophisticated expertise for moving minds onto the buying path created by using a well-designed plan of media advertising.

I knew that same behavior changing power could be put to work to change our behaviors for the good. We have already used national advertising campaigns for good - to teach, "Don't Drink and Drive," and "Prevent Forest Fires," and more recently, due to COVID, to "Wear Masks and Social Distance."

Once they are created by a relatively small staff, ads are disseminated to millions of people through the multiplying power of repetition in multi-media messaging. Media is the world's most cost-effective way to change behaviors. Once the investment has been made in the creativity and production of the "message," it can be duplicated and multiplied infinitely – as long as you have the money to pay for the media. Social media spreads its messages through becoming popular and "going viral' because many people become interested and post and share.

Short media messaging can be indefinitely replicated as far and as wide as your media budget will take it. I saw that changing behavior to improve our common good could be advertised in this way, just like products. My life changed as I saw my marketing career expertise and my passion for motivating us all to get along better – all come together.

In 1988, after my youngest son left for college, I moved away from Ohio, to take a job near Somerset, PA as the Marketing Director of a ski/golf resort named Hidden Valley. The former owner, George Parke, was a widower who was among the many friendly people I met while becoming acclimated to my new job and new home in Pennsylvania.

A year or so later, George and I began dating and eventually married in 1991. Early in our blooming friendship, I explained to him that I'd had this vision that we could uplift the community climate by publishing 12 habit-forming actions, each one "branded" by the name of a month as a symbol.

George liked the idea. As a respected business member of the Somerset community, he invited a group of civic leaders and youth to gather at Hidden Valley so I could explain the concept and how it might benefit the community. After the presentation to about 50 citizens, they all agreed that they'd like to try it in Somerset.

Fifteen community members then agreed to work together with George and me. We met monthly to determine the good values habits that would be used for each month. With the help of art students and the local printer, we designed, wrote and printed posters and flyers for local merchant stores, placemats for restaurants, bookmarks for schools, and newspaper editorials. We also

Students and volunteers preparing to install the new "Spirit of All of Us" lighted sculpture at Somerset, PA's Community Day in 1993. The sculpture is by metal artist, Dave Weimer, who also did a sculpture for the 911 Memorial for flight 93 in Shanksville, PA.

arranged for 30-second local radio spots about each month's habit, all written and recorded by students.

Community members created special events to re-enforce the monthly habits and to encourage community togetherness and cooperation. One was a FREE "All of Us - Appreciation Lunch," in May, where community leaders and volunteers cooked and served to everyone else.

For "Become Involved" in July, Somerset initiated a "Community Day" on the extra-large high school football field. All non-profits and faith groups were invited, free of charge, to set up booths with fun activities and to raise money for their charities. The date was coordinated with the annual fireworks show. About ½ hour before the fireworks, everyone was given a songbook of patriotic and old favorite songs, and went to the football stands to join a local bar-bershop quartet group in singing together.

After nearly 3 years, it was time to measure how the Somerset initiative was doing. A community-wide random phone survey was conducted by an Indiana University of Pennsylvania team of marketing graduate students. Their independently tabulated results proved that more than half the area population of 30,000 was already aware of All of Us. 72% of aware citizens said they were beginning to feel more warmth, unity and neighborly togetherness on a daily basis.

Most exciting of all is that 39% of the respondents said they had seen a habit message and actually improved their own behaviors at least once. These results were not from random ideas going viral. The results were motivated by a 12-month managed message social marketing/ advertising plan - and it WORKED.

As a result, at the end of 1993, the project, then called "All of Us," was designated as a Social Invention by the London Institute for Social Inventions and I was identified as a pioneer in the field of driving positive social engagement with a multi-media managed message campaign.

In the many years since Somerset, the 12 habit-building campaign grew to include many communities in western Pennsylvania including Pittsburgh where we were awarded a proclamation by the Pittsburgh City Council. Eight more survey studies were conducted primarily in schools, documenting that reading and math scores improved and detentions declined as much as 62% in one year in one school.

Outcomes statistically proved our campaign moved community-wide behaviors toward becoming more uplifted and unified. The REAL exciting outcomes were, and will always be, the inspired stories of people engaging their own ingenuity and creativity to bring alive each month's habit in personalized ways.

Everyone in all the schools and communities over the years loved to create their own ways to observe these 12 Habits celebrations. That's what is so neat about how the "12 Months to a Stronger America" plan works. This is why it motivates the hearts and souls of all of us to come together – each in our own creative way - one month at a time.

I will share here, a few of my favorite monthly inspired stories that I've experienced over the years. Remember, that because the messaging materials did the motivating, I was rarely present to experience much of the good that was being inspired.

Here, I am sharing just a few of the stories I experienced personally or learned about. Hopefully they will spark and motivate your own ideas for you to share with others as in "Pay It Forward." Of course, if you want to just read and enjoy the daily magic minutes, that's fine too.

Inspired Stories:

I'll begin this section with my very favorite story from Somerset, where, by 1993, the Monthly Habits had already become well-known among the residents. In February that year, a nearby ski resort was holding a Special Olympics Winter Sports Event.

It was being held in February, the month to celebrate that "You Count." The All of Us 12 Habits Team in the schools wanted to do something that would empower every child in the school system to become equally involved and to know that they counted in support of this big high profile community event.

This year, we wanted to honor February's habit "You Count" by including every single one of the nearly 2,500 students in the county. It was a seemingly impossible feat to achieve.

Early in November at a school staff meeting, a brilliant light-bulb went off in the creative center of one teacher's mind. She exclaimed, "Let's work with the District's Reading and English staff to create a special writing project for every student in every grade. The assignment will be to write a personal letter of welcome to each Special Olympian who will arrive in our community in February."

Everyone loved the idea. It wasn't difficult to get the rest of the staff on board. Several weeks before the Olympians arrived, the letter-writing assignment was given to all 2,500 students. The local newspaper, the Daily American, became involved and visited the schools to talk with students about the topics of their letters.

Several days before the event, all the student letters were collected and sorted into big brown envelopes with the name of each participating Olympian printed neatly on top. Some amazingly inspired letters included artwork, poetry and stories. Several art classes even decorated the envelopes.

Then during the Opening Day Ceremony in February, the bright-faced Special Olympians paraded around the open grounds near the ski lodge and viewing stands. At the end of the parade, each

Olympian was personally handed a large thick envelope containing at least a hundred delightful letters of welcome from ALL the students in Somerset County.

Yes, every student had counted. Unexpectedly, the local attendance at the Special Olympics Games was much higher than usual. A significant factor in the nearly doubled attendance was because many students were there with their families to greet and talk with the Olympians. A few students even found and sparked jubilant friendships with the Olympians who had received their letters.

The February inspiration in Somerset to make every student feel "counted" resulted in the success of a great day of happiness for every student, instead of just the few who usually represented the schools. From the motivation to fulfill the habit, "You Count," for every student, came an idea sparked by the genius light-bulb thought of just one person.

Just for you to enjoy and be inspired by the miraculous ingenuity residing in the hearts and minds of everyone around you, I'll additionally share some real actions inspired by the 12 Unity Habits in communities and schools over the last 30 years.

> KDKA-TV in Pittsburgh created and aired the 12 Habits as 30-second public service announcements. The spots aired for nearly three years and spawned growth of the 12 Habits into the Pittsburgh schools and into many western PA schools. These spots are now on YouTube at https://www.youtube.com/watch?v=0Wcp8oRwGvl&t=69s

> The Mayor of Cuyahoga Falls, OH, while at a crowded baseball game, remembered March's Habit "Resolve Conflicts." With great restraint he resisted the instinct to become outraged at someone in the crowd who accidentally spilled beer all over him.

> An adjudicated juvenile offender at South Hills Middle School near Pittsburgh, PA found and returned a checkbook to the school office because he had promised to "Do His Best" in September.

> An older couple, after many years of mutual indifference, decided to start holding hands again.

A dental group put each month's Habits posters on the ceilings over their patient's dental chairs.

A grocery store printed one of the 12 Monthly Habit themes each month, at the top of their sales receipts.

A local utility company inserted Monthly Habit reminders into their billing envelopes.

A restaurant made 12 Monthly Habit place mats, decorated with art from kids.

A second-grade teacher wrote a 12 Monthly Habits "Home Involvement Booklet" to help parents at home, practice the habits with their children.

A music teacher paid tribute to Mr. Rogers with a musical performance linking Mr. Rogers' songs to each month's Habit.

At Maplewood High School in Guys Mills, PA, school-wide monthly participation in 12 Monthly Caring Habits led to a Bronze Designation by US News and World Report in 2016.

> Louise Rice, Media Center Director, at Maplewood, produced numerous adventurous student-created videos of the 12 Monthly Habits in action in the school. There are seven on YouTube. Put "Caring Habits Louise Rice" into your YouTube browser. They're full of music and color and are worth looking at as an example of the power of the 12 Habits to inspire creativity among community residents, school students and staff.

A service organization in Oil City, PA made "screen savers" for their staff desk computers as 12 Habits reminders for staff.

A blind special education teacher/musician was inspired to write 12 songs, one song about each of the 12 habit themes.

A bus driver wrote a "Spirit of ALL of US" 12 Habits Newsletter and distributed it to all the transportation employees in Eugene, OR.

A community newspaper editor wrote a monthly feature article about one resident who most exemplifies each month's habit.

A community group held a poetry contest and had a "Get involved in Your Community" volunteer recruitment day.

A community newspaper, the Steel Valley Mirror, printed each month's Habit theme in the little extra spaces between articles throughout the paper.

20,000 Monthly Habits flyers focused on the health messages were printed by a local hospital and distributed by their employees throughout their community each month.

An Oil City, PA school invited community and parent "guests" to come to the school to read the daily habit from the Golden Rule book on morning announcements for all the students.

School children in Jeanette, PA made 12 Habit posters each month for distribution and display in local store windows and other public spaces.

A Senior Center in Berkeley Springs WV, baked and shared a "Resolve Conflicts" cake in March to help address the bickering issues that had become a problem.

In 2016, Educator/Songwriter, Dr. Melvin Steals autographs his classic recording, "Could It Be I'm Falling In Love," for former Warm Springs Middle School Principal, Gene Brock. The event was a 12 habits all-school rally for September, to "Do Your Best," held in Morgan County, WV. Dr. Steals was a visiting dignitary as the principal of the first school to implement the 12 Habits in Aliquippa, PA in 2000.

A coordinated "Parent Handbook" about Drug and Alcohol Abuse was written and distributed relating the 12 Habits to drug prevention behaviors and attitudes

A "Teen Center Without Walls" Calendar of Activities around the community for teens was published in the Somerset Daily American once a month.

A Home Economics class in Maplewood High School in Gates Mills, PA, made a patterned quilt of all twelve habits to exhibit in the school hallway and later raffled it off to help a student's family with medical bills. They also baked a "Be Appreciative" cake to honor the teachers in May.

In one High School, after a video and having discussions about micro-loans to encourage entrepreneurism in Rwanda, the Senior class voted to raise money to purchase a sewing machine for a Rwandan seamstress who I had met on my Rotary sponsored trip.

Because these are just the stories that I personally became aware of, the list above likely represents less than 5% of all the creative ideas and activities inspired by the 12 habits in several hundred schools and communities over thirty years.

These stories exemplify bringing us all together in unity and bringing out the best in everyone just like coming together to help in times of disaster does. This is how shared positive values practices, like rituals and holidays, work to motivate joy and creativity in a harmoniously shared single point in time – a day, a week, or a month.

The Rotary International sponsored 3-week peacekeeping trip to Rwanda in 2006, was one of my personal highlights of the many years so far, I have spent sharing the 12 habits monthly campaign with others. In 2005, our 12 habits initiative was displayed at Rotary's 100th Anniversary International Conference held in Chicago.

The delegation from Rwanda was at the conference looking for a "sponsor" project to inspire their youth to maintain peaceful relationships with one another to forever avoid another genocide like they had in 1994. At the time, Rwanda's national motto was, "Never Again."

The Rwandan Rotary Clubs coordinated with Rotary International,

Rotarian and author Elaine Parke, speaking about her peacekeeping trip to Rwanda to a Rotary Club near Pittsburgh, PA. She is wearing a Rwandan sari, and the Caring Habits logo for Rwanda is on the podium in front of her.

the Rwandan URC (National Unity and Reconciliation Commission), and the Ministry of Education to arrange my trip to share the 12 Monthly Caring Habits curriculum with Rwandan educators. I arrive at Kigali International Airport in late October, 2006 where I was joined by an escort from the NURC and an interpreter, who was the daughter of one of the Rotarians who first initiated the project, John Nyombayire.

It would take a full chapter to share my heart-warming stories about the amazing people of Rwanda who I encountered; so kind and gentle and strong and dignified, despite enduring the massive losses of the genocide only twelve short years before. Their national peace and unification projects were extensive and deeply dedicated to a future of happiness and unified prosperity for all Rwandans. Today, Rwanda is a leading country in the south-central region of Africa.

As you, my readers, now begin your own Unity Habits 12-month, "one minute a day" adventure, you'll see how each of the habits not only reinforce one another, but how they organically generate creative individual expressions and are self-sustaining.

This book holds an answer to how we can make the old Golden Rule mental health story new, and more powerful to influence all of us to unify us as a nation more than ever before. Like Rwanda, we can come back from stressful division to a more unified nation, more focused on the qualities of happy living and personal contentment, that we all share.

365 HABIT-BUILDING MOTIVATIONALS

...one month at a time

The 12 Mental Health Habits —
we will use to uplift ourselves and
heal the country we share.

January is Month 1

HELP OTHERS

*IN **JANUARY**... and all year long...*

Color Cue — Gentle Aqua

Health Focus — Learn CPR and First Aid

Daily Affirmation – TODAY, I offer my habit to HELP OTHERS

"Together we heal the country we all share"

— Elaine Parke

In JANUARY REMEMBER TO...
HELP OTHERS AND LEND A HAND

January is the beginning of a fresh new year and a great time to carry on the spirit of holiday giving. This month, when you see the color aqua, Gentle Aqua that is, think of how valuable you are, and that you can help others each day, even with just a smile. You might also plan to learn CPR and more about first aid so you are prepared to help someone when you least expect it.

Whether you have made a New Year's resolution or not, please read and sign the "January Promise" below. It is a lovely treasure I found on this "Becoming Unity in America" journey.

"Help Others" is celebrated in January, because it is right after the holiday season. December's hopeful holiday spirit of celebration and good will just ends abruptly. Now, all together, we are keeping the holiday "giving" mood going in January by promoting the ideal to "Help Others."

"Gentle Aqua" is a color to remind us of compassion and caring as it calms the nervous system. Check out your wardrobe and wear a little "aqua" during January.

THE JANUARY "HELP OTHERS" PROMISE*

I promise to be tender with the young,

Compassionate with the aging,

Sympathetic with the striving,

And tolerant with the weak and the wrong...

Because sometime in my life,

I will have been ALL of these!

My Name _____ Date _____

*The words of this Promise, from an unknown contributor, were allegedly printed in the Washington Post many years ago.

Goal for the Month:
To lift our spirits and the spirits of others by caring, sharing and giving.

Strengthening the positive in each of us. Enhancing community life for all.
— **Elaine Parke, Author**

In January, remember to ... Help Others.

Do all the good you can,
By all the means you can,
In all the ways you can,
In all the places you can,
At all the times you can,
To all the people you can,
As long as ever you can.

— **John Wesley**

Lend a Hand at helping others float - in the Heritage Festival Parade in Oil City, PA. There were 12 flatbed floats, one for each of the 12 months and each was decorated by a different local non-profit agency or organization. If this were in color you would see that everyone is wearing "gentle aqua" shirts.

JANUARY 1

TODAY.... I offer my habit to HELP OTHERS

THANK YOURSELF for taking the time to read a small part of this book every day. Appreciate yourself for being determined to make the UNITY HABITS more active in your life than ever before. This short poem is a great reminder and a compass for daily thinking.

> *To look up and not down*
> *To look forward and not back*
> *To look out and not in, and*
> *To lend a hand.*
> — **Edward Everett Hale, American Author**

Plan to hold a "Help Others" party this month. You might ask everyone to bring an item of food for the needy and to bring their own stories about helping others and about being helped. Notice the mood of the gathering. Isn't it great?!

HELP OTHERS *in January*

HABITS FOR UNITY   **Aqua**

JANUARY 2

TODAY.... I offer my habit to HELP OTHERS

We live in a fast-paced and "over-busy" world where, like horses with blinders, our "to-do" lists and "must-dos" block us from noticing the needs of others around us. Stopping to be helpful takes just minutes from our day and the joy received is timeless. It's taken just 60 seconds to read this, so you still have time today to be kind.

> *If you stop to be kind, you must swerve often from your path.*
> — **Mary Webb, Author, Precious Bane**

> *Happiness is the by-product of helping others.*
> — **Denny Miller**

Be watchful today for someone who needs help and a minute of your time.

JANUARY 3
TODAY.... I offer my habit to HELP OTHERS

Life is in the little things. Think about what pleased you yesterday. Did a co-worker smile as you passed in the hall? Did you find a flower bud or a new shoot on one of your house plants? Did you get an unexpected hug at home?

> *Life is not so short but that there is always time enough for giving courtesy.*
> **— Ralph Waldo Emerson, American Poet and Essayist**

> *The difference between a helping hand and an outstretched palm is a twist of the wrist.*
> **— Lawrence Leamer, Author**

Leave a treat and a note of thanks for your newspaper or mail delivery person.

HABITS FOR UNITY   Aqua

HELP OTHERS *in January*

JANUARY 4
TODAY.... I offer my habit to HELP OTHERS

Life happens in little moments. You have power over how they add up. Think about each moment today. The great equalizer is that everyone has 1,440 minutes a day. Live today by making a memory and a treasure out of each moment.

> *Little deeds of kindness,*
> *Little words of love*
> *Help to make earth happy*
> *Like the heaven above.*
> **— Julia A. Fletcher Carney**

> *In this world, you must be a bit too kind in order to be kind enough.*
> **— Pierre Carlet de Chamblain de Marivaux**

Give a parking break. Let someone in ahead of you with a smile. Smile and thank every store clerk who takes care of you today.

JANUARY 5

TODAY.... I offer my habit to HELP OTHERS

None of us can appreciate life and one another as deeply as someone who has lost theirs and then miraculously returned to life.

> *We are powerful spiritual beings meant to create good on the earth. This good isn't usually accomplished in bold actions, but in singular acts of kindness between people. It's the little things that count, because they are more spontaneous and show who you truly are. I am elated. I now know the simple secret to improving mankind. The amount of love and good feelings you have at the end of your life is equal to the love and good feelings you put out during your life.*
> — **Danion Brinkley, Author, Saved by the Light**

Find some "singular act of kindness" that you can do for another— hug your child or your spouse, or a friend.
Only you know.

HABITS FOR UNITY   **HELP OTHERS** *in January*   **Aqua**

JANUARY 6

TODAY.... I offer my habit to HELP OTHERS

What is wisdom? How wise are we, even with thousands of years of recorded history to learn from? What kind of progress have we made toward equality and justice for all? Are you wise? What does progress mean to you?

> *Civilization is just the slow process of learning to be kind.*
> — **Will Durant**

> *Kindness is more important than wisdom, and the recognition of this is the beginning of wisdom.*
> — **Theodore Isaac Rubin, M.D and Author, One to One**

> *What wisdom can you find that is greater than kindness?*
> — **Jean Jacques Rousseau**

Tell your bus driver how much you appreciate their driving. Perhaps your "bus driver" is your spouse, or your mom or dad, or a friend.

JANUARY 7
TODAY.... I offer my habit to HELP OTHERS

As you go through your day, pay special attention to the people you interact with. If you notice someone is irritable or aloof, try to look for a reason to feel compassion rather than criticism or blame.

> *Two important things are to have a genuine interest in people and to be kind to them. Kindness, I've discovered, is everything in life.*
> — Isaac Bashevis, Singer and Jewish-American Author

> *There's more power in the open hand than in the clenched fist.*
> — Martin Luther King, Jr.

Today, I will give a note to someone offering to help them. I already know who needs this note from me.

HABITS FOR UNITY   Aqua

JANUARY 8
TODAY.... I offer my habit to HELP OTHERS

How do you make a living?

> *From what we get, we make a living; what we give, however, makes a life.*
> — Arthur Ashe, American Tennis Player, Author, Days of Grace

> *You've got to give to get. And if you don't plan on givin', then you better not plan on gettin'.*
> — Joe Clark

Be a buddy or friend to a new co-worker, a new neighbor, or a new student at school. Show them you notice them and demonstrate a genuine interest in learning about them.

JANUARY 9

TODAY…. I offer my habit to HELP OTHERS

What is success?

> *Success has nothing to do with what you gain in life or accomplish for yourself. It's what you do for others.*
> — **Danny Thomas, Actor-Comedian**

> *You roll my log, and I will roll yours.*
> — **Seneca Indian Saying**

> *We're not primarily put on this earth to see through one another, but to see one another through.*
> — **Peter De Vries, Author, Let Me Count the Ways**

Before you go to bed tonight, write your personal definition of success. Think about what success means in your life and what you hope to leave as your legacy someday.

HABITS FOR UNITY   **HELP OTHERS** in January   **Aqua**

JANUARY 10

TODAY…. I offer my habit to HELP OTHERS

People need our help and so does our environment, our plants, and our animals. "Help Others," therefore, also applies to helping save birds and animals and our planet when we can. I have a friend who once said, "Help everyone; and if you can't help, at least don't hurt them." We can all help by not hurting our environment.

> *What we must decide is how we are valuable rather than how valuable we are.*
> — **Edgar Z. Friedenberg**

> *You give but little when you give your possessions. It is when you give of yourself that you truly give.*
> — **Kahlil Gibran**

Hang a bird feeder and keep it filled. Give treats to your own pet or a favorite pet belonging to someone else—even if the treat is only a pat or a hug of affection. Send a contribution to save the habitat of an endangered species.

JANUARY 11*

TODAY…. I offer my habit to HELP OTHERS

Joy is a gift you give to yourself and others. Even if you have troubles and you don't feel like it—fake it for a while and see what happens. Give a smile and good cheer to everyone you see—from the moment you open your eyes in the morning until you close them again at night. Smiles, joy and music are my favorite things.

> *Smiles are wondrous things; you can give them out for eternity and still have one left for yourself.*
> — **Colleen, Age 13 – "The Peanut Butter Gang"**

> *A smile is the beginning of peace.*
> — **Mother Teresa**

Hum a few happy tunes today. Here are several you may know.

"I Gotta Feeling," by the Black Eyed Peas,

"Beautiful Day," by U2,

"Ain't No Mountain High Enough," by Marvin Gaye,

"When You're Smiling," by Judy Garland,

"Don't Stop Believing," by Journey,

"Service with a Smile," by Cheryl Prewitt-Salem,

"Zip-a-Dee-Do-Dah,"
 from Song of the South.

HABITS FOR UNITY   Aqua

* Today is my own birthday.

Here, I am happily resting my feet on a cooler in a canoe on the Allegheny River in northern Pennsylvania. I am also happy that you are here, reading about "Helping Others" during January.

JANUARY 12

TODAY.... I offer my habit to HELP OTHERS

I read somewhere that the healing power of prayer has been scientifically proven. No matter what you believe, try sending positive prayers or thoughts to someone you know who is experiencing pain or grief.

> *He who prays for his neighbor will be heard for himself.*
> — **Talmud, Jewish Holy Book**

> *Kindliness antedates psychiatry by hundreds of years; its antiquity should not lessen your opinion of its usefulness.*
> — **Dr. J. Roswell Gallagher**

> *Make yourself necessary to somebody.*
> — **Ralph Waldo Emerson**

If you have an elderly neighbor, check-in on them today.
Pray that their needs will be met.
Who else needs your prayers today?

HABITS FOR UNITY   Aqua

JANUARY 13

TODAY.... I offer my habit to HELP OTHERS

Spend today acknowledging how other peoples' lives are intertwined with your own. Look around you. Ask yourself who made the chair you're sitting on. Think about who picked the potato you're having for dinner. Think about who stocked the shelves at the grocery store.

> *We seldom stop to think how many peoples' lives are entwined with our own. It is a form of selfishness to imagine that everyone can operate on his own or can pull out of the general stream and not be missed.*
> — **Ivy Baker Priest, Former US Treasurer**

Write a note to a person from your past who intertwined their life with yours when you needed it and made a difference. Give them the gift of appreciation.

JANUARY 14
TODAY.... I offer my habit to HELP OTHERS

One of my observations is that we try to substitute words for actions when it comes to making a better world. We can talk a good line when it comes to telling others what to do but the question is: "Do we walk the talk?"

Words are plentiful, but deeds are precious.
— **Lech Walensa, Former Polish Prime Minister**

The impersonal hand of government can never replace the helping hand of a neighbor.
— **Hubert H. Humphrey, Former Vice-President of the US**

TODAY: Walk the talk. Remember the three "Rs" — Regard for self; Respect for others, Responsibility for all your actions.

HABITS FOR UNITY   **HELP OTHERS** *in January*   Aqua

JANUARY 15
TODAY.... I offer my habit to HELP OTHERS

How many books or poems or stories do you read about the pleasures of making and spending lots of money? There are none that I know of because human contentment and happiness are always about people's compassion and kindness.

Happiness is the by-product of helping others.
— **Denny Miller**

If I can stop one heart from breaking
I shall not live in vain
If I can ease one life the aching
Or cool one pain
Or help one fainting robin unto his nest again
I shall not live in vain.
— **Emily Dickinson, American Poet**

Help others by showing gratitude. Thank your spouse, child, friend, boss, secretary, or teacher for the things they do and have done for you.

JANUARY 16

TODAY…. I offer my habit to HELP OTHERS

Practicing random acts of kindness became popular because giving became an event—a series of great and wonderful surprises. There was a tradition practiced at the concert gates of the 1960's band The Grateful Dead. People would buy an extra ticket and give it to a "ticket-in-need" stranger outside the gate. This tradition was called "miracling."

> *The love we give away is the only love we keep.*
> — **Elbert Hubbard, Author, The Notebook of Elbert Hubbard**

> *God speaks wherever He finds a humble, listening ear. And the language He uses is Kindness.*
> — **Lena Horne, Singer-Actress**

Give a stranger a ticket to a sports event or a concert.

HABITS FOR UNITY   **Aqua**

JANUARY 17

TODAY…. I offer my habit to HELP OTHERS

Nourishment is easily recognized in the form of food. Kind words and caring stories are also nourishment. A once-popular self-help book series is called "Chicken Soup" because food is a symbol of caring. We share food when a family loses a loved one, or when there is illness, or simply to welcome the arrival of a new neighbor.

> *Who gives to the poor gives to God.*
> — **Victor Hugo**

> *We must strive to multiply bread so that it suffices for the tables of mankind.*
> — **Pope John Paul II**

Bring a large batch of your "best recipe" homemade cookies to a homeless shelter. Offer to volunteer there. Find out what other help you can provide.

JANUARY 18

TODAY…. I offer my habit to HELP OTHERS

Show everyone you meet today that you care about them while you are with them. Whether a store clerk, a co-worker with a problem, or a child with a bad attitude, look at them and really listen when they talk. Let them know you think they are an important and valuable person.

> *People want to know how much you care before they care how much you know.*
> — **James F. Hind, The Wall Street Journal**

> *Friendship is the pleasing game of interchanging praise.*
> — **Oliver Wendell Holmes, American Author**

Actually, say the words, "I care about you" to someone.

HABITS FOR UNITY   **Aqua**

JANUARY 19

TODAY…. I offer my habit to HELP OTHERS

Do you have charity in your heart today? Share your heart full of charity. Invite someone to join you in attending your place of worship or a service organization where you know there is warmth and caring.

> *If you haven't any charity in your heart, you have the worst kind of heart trouble.*
> — **Bob Hope, Actor-Comedian**

> *A real friend is one who helps us think our best thoughts, do our noblest deeds, and be our finest selves.*
> — **Anonymous**

Give people more than they expect, and do it cheerfully.

JANUARY 20

TODAY.... I offer my habit to HELP OTHERS

Look for the secret that sparks joy and motivates someone you love. Ignite that spark with your words or your actions.

Every human being has some hand by which he may be lifted, some groove in which he was meant to run; and the great work of life, as far as our relations with each other are concerned, is to lift each one by his own proper handle, and run each one in his own proper groove.
— **Harriet Beecher Stowe, Author, Little Foxes**

The entire sum of existence is the magic of being needed by just one person.
—**Vi Putnam, Author, Hard Hearts Are for Cabbages**

Live a good and nourishing life. Then when you get older and think back, you'll get to enjoy it twice.

HABITS FOR UNITY   Aqua

JANUARY 21

TODAY.... I offer my habit to HELP OTHERS

Expect a miracle today. Look in the mirror. Hold up your hand. Look carefully at your own face and your own hand. You are the miracle. Surely there is a miraculous kindness that you can bestow on another.

The miracle is this -- the more we share, the more we have.
— **Leonard Nimoy, Actor**

When friends ask me when the (Quaker) Service is – I tell them that service comes after the (Quaker) Meeting.
— **William Penn, Founder of Pennsylvania**

You can give the gift of laughter today. You are a miracle. If you know a joke, tell it to someone who needs a joke.

JANUARY 22
TODAY.... I offer my habit to HELP OTHERS

Look through today's local newspaper headlines. Notice stories where people have been hurt or sustained a loss. Think about how you would feel if this had happened to you. Consider doing something to help. Call the newspaper or TV station, or the police, to find out what you can do.

> *A community is not a place. It begins in thought, and in the heart and spirit. Community is in the climate of empathy.*
> — **Elaine Parke, Author**

> *The worst prison would be a closed heart.*
> — **Pope John Paul II**

Give the tools of courage to someone who needs them — perhaps someone whose story is in the newspaper.

HABITS FOR UNITY   *HELP OTHERS in January*   **Aqua**

JANUARY 23
TODAY.... I offer my habit to HELP OTHERS

Contact someone today you don't "think" you like very well. Convey a compliment or a positive message. If you feel awkward at first, tell them you think they have great elbows or that you know they keep a very neat medicine chest. I'm sort of kidding a bit, but you get the point.

> *The heart is the toughest part of the body.*
> — **Carolyn Forché, Author, The Country Between Us**

> *The only thing we can offer of value is to give our love to people as unworthy of it as we are of God's love.*
> — **St. Catherine of Sienna**

At the end of the day, ask yourself how you feel now about a person you spent time with that day. Did you add to their day?

JANUARY 24

TODAY.... I offer my habit to HELP OTHERS

Really LOOK at your HAND today. Hold it open. Think about the times in your life so far that you've extended a helping hand to others. Imagine how good the giving feels. Bask in the warmth of knowing that you care.

> *A man there was, though some did count him mad, the more he cast away, the more he had.*
> — **John Bunyan**

> *The best place to find a helping hand is at the end of your arm.*
> — **Elmer Letterman**

> *A hand up is better than a hand out.*
> — **Sybil Mobley**

Watch your own hand give a cookie to a child or a cup of coffee to a coworker.

HABITS FOR UNITY   Aqua

JANUARY 25

TODAY.... I offer my habit to HELP OTHERS

Write a letter of satisfaction (instead of a complaint letter) to the boss of someone who has helped you. Imagine being in the room when the boss tells this employee he/she has received your letter. Imagine what the boss will say. Do you think the employee will get a raise?

> *I hope, when I stop, people will think that somehow, I mattered.*
> — **Martina Navratilova, Women's Tennis Champion**

Write a note to your spouse or a loved one.
You know what to say.

JANUARY 26
TODAY.... I offer my habit to HELP OTHERS

Take to heart the quote below that service is the rent we pay to live here on earth. The reverse of that thought is what I often observe; that I get more happiness and joy when I help someone than perhaps what I give to them. Give a little today. Feel the warmth.

> *I expect to pass through life but once. If therefore, there be any kindness I can show, or any good thing I can do to any fellow being, let me do it now, and not defer or neglect it, as I shall not pass this way again.*
> — **William Penn, Founder of Pennsylvania**

> *Service is the rent you pay for room on this earth.*
> — **Shirley Chisolm, Former US Congresswoman**

Do someone else's job at home tonight—
do the dishes, take out
the garbage, walk the dog....

HABITS FOR UNITY   Aqua

JANUARY 27
TODAY.... I offer my habit to HELP OTHERS

> *It's not what we give, but what we share—For the gift without the giver is bare; Who gives himself with his alms feeds three— himself, his hungering neighbor, and Me.*
> — **James Russell Lowell, American Poet**

> *The manner of giving is worth more than the gift.*
> — **Pierre Corneille**

> *Give what you have. To someone, it may be better than you dare think.*
> — **Henry Wadsworth Longfellow, Poet**

Take a plate of cookies or a cheerful plant to the police
or fire department.

JANUARY 28

TODAY.... I offer my habit to HELP OTHERS

If you haven't used "it" in two years, then donate it or take it to a recycle facility. Have you ever seen a U-Haul truck in a funeral procession? Have you ever seen the happy face of a child, on a cold day, with a new (to him/her) coat?

> *No one may forsake his neighbor when he is in trouble. Everybody is under obligation to help and support his neighbor as he would himself like to be helped.*
> — Martin Luther

> *One can give nothing whatever without giving oneself—that is to say, risking oneself. If not risk oneself, then one is simply incapable of giving.*
> — James Baldwin, American Author

Can you risk giving away something you haven't used lately but may need someday?

HABITS FOR UNITY   **HELP OTHERS** in January   **Aqua**

JANUARY 29

TODAY.... I offer my habit to HELP OTHERS

What would happen to "road rage" if all drivers were courteous and kind to one another? Give another driver a good parking spot that you saw before they did. Notice the look on their face when they realize what you are doing. Later in the day, let someone pull in front of you who is waiting to enter a thoroughfare.

> *One can never pay in gratitude; one can only pay "in kind" somewhere else in life.*
> — Anne Morrow Lindbergh, Author, North to the Orient

> *Kindness consists in loving people more than they deserve.*
> — Joseph Joubert

Decide to be a courteous driver today—again tomorrow— and again, the day after that.

JANUARY 30
TODAY.... I offer my habit to HELP OTHERS

It's almost the end of January, but not the end of the need to help and support one another. You can give away a million dollars or an hour of your time or you can give a smile. Each of these gifts is important.

> *Find out where you can render a service, and then render it.*
> — **S.S. Kresge, American Merchant**

> *The greatest comfort of my old age, and that which gives me the highest satisfaction, is the pleasing remembrance of the many benefits and friendly offices I have done to others.*
> — **Cato**

Make a pledge to keep your giving spirit going.

HABITS FOR UNITY   Aqua

JANUARY 31
TODAY.... I offer my habit to HELP OTHERS

Tomorrow, we start enjoying the Unity Habit, "You Count." Remember that you "count" most when you lend a hand to others. Opportunities to help others are as small and effortless as a smile. Keep your hand open and the thought of "Help Others" in your heart as you begin the month of February and the Unity Habit "You Count."

> *He who waits to do a great deal of good at once will never do anything.*
> — **Samuel Johnson**

> *Great opportunities to help others seldom come, but small ones surround us every day.*
> — **Sally Koch**

Softly, to yourself, say the words, "peace begins with me." I can give a smile that is heartfelt, spontaneous, and free.

February is Month 2

YOU COUNT

*IN **FEBRUARY**... and all year long...*

Color Cue — WOW! Fuchsia

Health Focus — Be Drug FREE

Affirmation – TODAY, I remind myself, YOU COUNT!!

"Together we heal the country we all share."

– Elaine Parke

In FEBRUARY, REMEMBER THAT...
YOU COUNT!!

This month's celebration color is WOW! Fuchsia. Whenever I see or wear the color Fuchsia, I will remember that I count and that I make a difference wherever I go.

In February, we celebrate Black History Month. This is because we want black Americans and Americans of every color to know that they are very important in the successful progress of our country. Feeling that "You Count" is to feel worthy, to know you have value, and know that you are good and have the power to do good.

One of the reasons I wrote this book is because it never made sense to me that some people valued some lives more than others based on silly physical differences. The habits in this book are all about the unifying qualities that we have in common. Focusing on these shared qualities inspire a whole lot more unity among us than emphasizing minor differences, blown way out of proportion.

When you know you count, you know you have a purpose and that you were born with gifts to fulfill that purpose. Each day we use our time, our thoughts, and our energy. Together we could turn all of us into humane beings more than just human beings. Humane beings are generous, democratic, forgiving, kind hearted, unselfish and amiable. Wouldn't that be great?

What is so exciting about being alive is that we affect our lives and the lives of others. This is why we are each too important to abuse ourselves with drugs and alcohol.

All of us together are the essence of community. Each one COUNTS! A farmer, a nurse, a teacher, and a grocery clerk each provide a necessary ingredient needed for the community to operate properly. We all count. In our homes and in our community, we all play a role in the group activity. This is how we feel joy and success in life.

Making a difference doesn't have to be a big deal. Look at the paper clip you may use today to hold paper sheets together.

Somebody made that paper clip! Right now, to you, that person counts. If that person hadn't made the paper clip, your papers would fall apart.

Survey your skills, your hopes and your dreams, and write them down. Do you have a dream you keep secret because you don't believe it could ever happen? Let the Daily Unity Habits work in your mind and in your heart this month. Re-dedicate yourself to you and to those around you.

We all count and count on others.
— Noah Ben Shea

Goal for the Month:
To know that you count and to BELIEVE it.

I am only one,
But still, I am one
I cannot do everything,
But still, I can do something;
And because I cannot do everything
I will not refuse to do the something that I can do.
— Edward Everett Hale, American Author

In February, remember—You Count!

Our deepest fear is not that we are inadequate. Our deepest fear is that we are powerful beyond measure. It is our light, not our darkness, that most frightens us. We ask ourselves, 'Who am I to be brilliant, gorgeous, talented and fabulous? Actually, who are you not to be?
— Nelson Mandela, Former President of South Africa,
   1994 inaugural speech

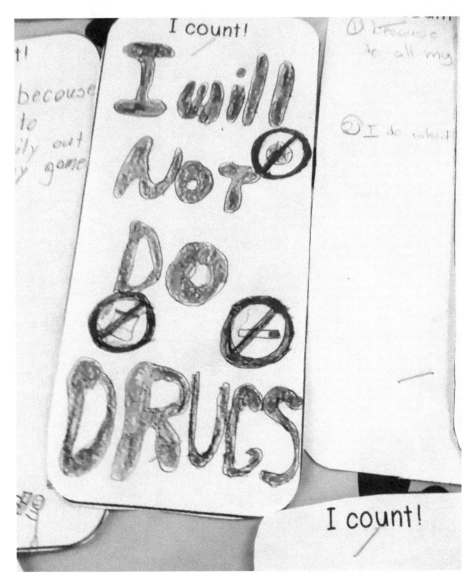

A February "YOU COUNT" activity at Warm Springs Middle School in Morgan County, WV, included a bulletin board with papers each student wrote about why, "I Count."

FEBRUARY 1

TODAY.... I remind myself - YOU COUNT

The following Booker T. Washington quote is one of my favorites. He understood that each one of us is important every moment of every day. We all have the ability to enrich and support one another or to tear one another down. Each day, you are given a bank account of 1,440 minutes. No person on Earth gets more than you do.

> *You've got to put your own bucket down where you are.*
> — **Booker T. Washington**

Today I'll do good.

HABITS FOR UNITY   CO**U**NT   Fuchsia

FEBRUARY 2

TODAY.... I remind myself - YOU COUNT

In the United States, February 2 is Groundhog Day. From a little town in western Pennsylvania, the groundhog, Punxsutawney Phil, counts! Legend has it that if the sun shines and Phil sees his shadow, we should expect six more weeks of winter weather.

> *You make a difference—every day—no matter what the weather. You need only claim the events of your life to make yourself yours.*
> — **Florida Scott-Maxwell, The Measure of My Days**

Today I'll be thoughtful and gentle with others.

FEBRUARY 3
TODAY.... I remind myself - YOU COUNT

This is Black History Month, when we remember that we all count—
no matter what our history or what our beliefs are. This is a month
to especially honor African Americans. The first quote for February is by Booker T. Washington, one of our great African American
historical contributors. Together, we all share the responsibility for
making this a better world. Even one smile helps someone.

> *Our flag is red, white, and blue, but our nation is a rainbow—*
> *red, yellow, brown, black and white—and we're all precious*
> *in God's sight.*
> — **Rev. Jesse Jackson, American Human Rights Activist**

> *America is not a melting pot—America is a beautiful mosaic.*
> — **Patt Derian, American Human Rights Activist**

Today, I'll do a great job.

HABITS FOR UNITY   **CO**U**NT**™ *in February*   Fuchsia

FEBRUARY 4
TODAY.... I remind myself - YOU COUNT

This is a wonderful month to remember that our children count,
too. "You Count" in the lives of children. If you have children at
home, spend extra time with them or with your grandchildren or
with the neighbor's children. Let children know you value and respect them. Encourage them to know they count.

> *Children don't learn...from people who don't love them.*
> — **General John Stafford, Seattle Public Schools**

> *Give a little love to a child and you get a great deal back.*
> — **John Ruskin, English Writer and Artist**

Today I'll be patient with children.

FEBRUARY 5

TODAY.... I remind myself, YOU COUNT

Becoming more self-reliant is another way to celebrate "You Count." Maybe you've wanted to learn more about handling your own finances or about calculating your taxes. Celebrate "You Count" by taking charge of a new aspect of your life.

> *You can count on others but it's better to use your own fingers and toes.*
> — **Bazooka Joe**

> *Always do what you say you are going to do. It is the glue and fiber that binds successful relationships.*
> — **Jeffrey A. Timmons, The Entrepreneurial Mind**

Today I'll find out how to do it myself and then do it.

HABITS FOR UNITY   CO**U**NT   Fuchsia
in February

FEBRUARY 6

TODAY.... I remind myself - YOU COUNT

We all have days when nothing seems to go right. Hopefully, today is not one of those days. Today, think about your own significance in the face of adversity. Whether it's your own or someone else's, you can be a part of the solution. For those who know they "count," the pains of living become the lessons of life.

> *Turn hurt into a halo, turn scars into stars.*
> — **Reverend Robert Schuller, American Clergyman**

> *There are victories of the soul and spirit. Sometimes, even if you lose, you win.*
> — **Elie Wiesel, Nobel Laureate and Holocaust Survivor**

Today I'll make lemonade out of lemons.

FEBRUARY 7
TODAY.... I remind myself - YOU COUNT

Who is the "YOU" that counts during this month of February? Invest a few minutes to take stock. You might even want to start a journal. Write down the moments each day when you know you counted—when you encouraged a friend, when you made a suggestion at work or school, or when you listened to a child.

> *You never find yourself until you face the truth.*
> — **Pearl Bailey, American Singer-Actress**

> *Not all of us have to possess earthshaking talent. Just common sense and love will do.*
> — **Myrtle Auvil, American Author**

Today, I'll take ten quiet moments with me.

HABITS FOR UNITY   Fuchsia

FEBRUARY 8
TODAY.... I remind myself - YOU COUNT

Have you ever lost a small screw out of a piece of equipment and found that the whole thing broke down? Just like a small screw, each one of us is holding something together in our own part of the world. As you go through your day today, think about this at home with your family, at work, or just out in the community.

> *Everybody has to be somebody to somebody to be anybody.*
> — **Malcolm S. Forbes, American Businessman**

> *When we turn to each other, and not on each other, that's victory.*
> — **Rev. Jesse Jackson, American Human Rights Activist**

Today, I'll call someone and ask them to share a meal.

FEBRUARY 9

TODAY.... I remind myself - YOU COUNT

Random Acts of Kindness Week is celebrated this month. Why is each of us unique and important? With your words and actions today, let the people around you know that you respect them and value their place in your life. Build them up; see their point of view; show kindness regularly as well as randomly. Show that you care.

> *Commandment Number One of any truly civilized society is this: Let people be different.*
> — **David Grayson, American Author**

> *Life is rather like a can of sardines—we're all looking for the key.*
> — **Alan Bennet, British Playwright**

Today, I'll tell each person why they are valuable to me.

HABITS FOR UNITY   **Fuchsia**

FEBRUARY 10

TODAY.... I remind myself - YOU COUNT

Do you ever feel small and unimportant? I know I do. This is the month to remember that every person is important. Each of us is needed by someone every day. How rich or how powerful we are is not a measure of importance. However, in today's society, we lose sight of this. What is the measure of importance in your life?

> *Even a small star shines in the darkness.*
> — **Finnish Proverb**

> *There is not enough darkness in the world to put out the light of even one small candle.*
> — **Robert Alder, Austrian Inventor**

Today, I'll find value in each thing I do.

FEBRUARY 11
TODAY.... I remind myself - YOU COUNT

February is American Heart Health Awareness month. One way to show yourself that "You Count" is to focus on your own health.

> *H elp other people*
> *E xercise regularly*
> *A void guns and violence*
> *L earn safety rules*
> *T ake time to rest*
> *H andwashing often*
> *I llegal drugs and alcohol are bad*
> *E at healthy foods*
> *R espect nature*
> – **Heather Dixon, a 4th grader in Bethel Park, PA:**

It's alright to drink like a fish if you drink what a fish drinks.
— **Mary Pettibone Poole, American Author**

HABITS FOR UNITY   Fuchsia

FEBRUARY 12
TODAY.... I remind myself - YOU COUNT

Today is Abraham Lincoln's Birthday. I sort of flinch at the concept of common-looking people. Who wants to look common? However, maybe Abe was on to something when he realized the truth about what is really important in life. From now on, I will regard common-looking as a badge of distinction.

> *Common-looking people are the best in the world: that is the reason the Lord makes so many of them.*
> — **Abraham Lincoln, 16th President of the US**

Today, I'll observe the people I see with a new respect for who they are.

FEBRUARY 13

TODAY.... I remind myself - YOU COUNT

There are those of us who are an exception. We march to a different drummer in a parade that is all our own. Many of us step out onto paths others will not first take—but upon which others will soon follow. Who is your drummer? Take courage in staying a course that you believe in and in following your truth. You Count.

How glorious it is—and how painful also—to be an exception.
— Alfred De Musset, French Novelist

If a man does not keep pace with his companions, it is perhaps because he hears a different drummer. Let him step to the music that he hears, however measured or far away.
— Henry David Thoreau, American Author

Today I'll take a different path home.

HABITS FOR UNITY   CO**U**NT   Fuchsia
in February

FEBRUARY 14

TODAY.... I remind myself - YOU COUNT

Love is the ultimate expression of "You Count." In America, this is Valentine's Day, the day we celebrate and honor love. Saint Valentine's Day was originally the Roman feast of Lupercalia, Christianized in memory of the martyr St. Valentine (A.D. 270). In the Middle Ages, St. Valentine became associated with the union of lovers under conditions of duress. Today, the holiday is celebrated with the exchange of romantic or comic messages called Valentines.

The supreme happiness of life is knowing we are loved.
— Victor Hugo, Author of Les Miserables

Today, I'll call or send Valentine greetings to everyone that I can.

FEBRUARY 15
TODAY.... I remind myself - YOU COUNT

You probably have a few Valentine's cards in your home today. Valentine's is such a great day of the year for bolstering our own sense of self-worth. Really cherish the cards you received this year. Think about the verses written on them and cherish the people who sent them to you. Immerse yourself in love.

> *No one can figure out your worth but you.*
> — **Pearl Bailey, American Singer and Actress**

> *Everybody is somebody.*
> — **Jesse Jackson, American Civil Rights Activist**

Today, I'll make myself some cookies
and then share them.

HABITS FOR UNITY   Fuchsia

FEBRUARY 16
TODAY.... I remind myself - YOU COUNT

This is a good day to prove to ourselves that we count. Count the number of minutes you have in a 24-hour day. Do you realize that time is the ultimate equalizer? Did you come up with 1,440 minutes like I did? How many times can you make a difference in 1,440 minutes? Have you ever thought about the fact that there is no one on earth who has more minutes each day than you do?

> *What we must decide is how we are valuable rather than how valuable we are.*
> — **Edgar Z. Friedenberg**

> *You have '1,440 POWER,' today and every day.*
> — **Elaine Parke, Author**

Today, I'll call someone and share
something positive about today.

FEBRUARY 17

TODAY.... I remind myself - YOU COUNT

We all count in this world, for better or for worse. We don't mean to cause "worse;" yet sometimes, even without knowing it, our words or actions hurt others. I remember the childhood ditty "sticks and stones." One way adults hurt each other with words is with gossip. Make a commitment today to stay away from gossip.

> *Sticks and stones may break our bones,*
> *but words will break our hearts.*
> — **Robert Fulghum, Author**

> *Frogs have it easy, they can eat what bugs them.*
> — **Author Unknown**

Today, I'll make a commitment to stay away from all gossip – even if someone bugs me.

HABITS FOR UNITY   CO**U**NT™   Fuchsia

FEBRUARY 18

TODAY.... I remind myself - YOU COUNT

"Trust" is a secular word for faith. When you have self-trust, you have faith and confidence in yourself and what you have to give to others. Self-trust is basic to the concept of "You Count." Go forth into your day with faith and trust.

> *Self-trust is the essence of heroism.*
> — **Ralph Waldo Emerson, Author and Poet**

> *Trust yourself, then you will know how to live.*
> — **Johannes Wolfgang von Goethe, German Writer**

Today, I'll remember to trust myself when I am tempted to please someone else against my own better judgment.

FEBRUARY 19
TODAY.... I remind myself - YOU COUNT

Remember those 1,440 minutes that you now know you have today? Like ants on a log, each minute seems tiny compared to large measures of time like a millennium. Think about a project you want to do that is overwhelming. Today, imagine that project is a pile of bricks that you place, one by one, into a structure that is the success you are looking for. It is beautiful, isn't it?

> *It is the greatest of all mistakes to do nothing because you can only do a little. Do what you can.*
> — **Sydney Smith, English Philosopher**

Today, I'll start something I've been putting off.

HABITS FOR UNITY   Fuchsia

FEBRUARY 20
TODAY.... I remind myself - YOU COUNT

This is a story about four people. Their names were Everybody, Somebody, Anybody and Nobody.

> *There was an important job to be done and*
> *Everybody was sure that Somebody would do it.*
>
> *Anybody could have done it, but Nobody did it.*
>
> *Somebody got angry about it because it was Everybody's job.*
>
> *Everybody thought Anybody could do it,*
> *but Nobody realized that Everybody wouldn't do it.*
>
> *It ended up that Everybody blamed Somebody,*
> *when Nobody did what Anybody could have done.*
> — **Anonymous**

Today, I'll be the one who does the job.

FEBRUARY 21

TODAY.... I remind myself - YOU COUNT

Step back from your day for a moment. Look at how all the unique people of the world work together to make things bloom and grow among us. You are one of all of us. The gift of you and your uniqueness adds to the life we share.

> *You are unique, and if that is not fulfilled,*
> *then something has been lost.*
> — **Martha Graham, American Dancer**

> *I make the most of all that comes and the least of all that goes.*
> — **Sara Teasdale, "The Philosopher"**

Today, I'll write myself a complimentary note
and post it where I can see it quite often.

HABITS FOR UNITY   CO**U**NT™   Fuchsia

FEBRUARY 22

TODAY.... I remind myself, YOU COUNT

Today is George Washington's Birthday. The strength of our democracy is based on this month's Unity Habit: "You Count." Do you honor your responsibility to vote? What other responsibilities do you have as a democratic citizen? With rights come responsibilities. Here is a reminder from the Declaration of Independence:

> *"We hold these truths to be self-evident; that all men are*
> *created equal; that they are endowed by their Creator with*
> *unalienable rights; that among these are life, liberty and the*
> *pursuit of happiness."*

Today, I'll think of George Washington and take personal responsibility for being a good citizen in my own life.

FEBRUARY 23
TODAY.... I remind myself, YOU COUNT

Why is it so difficult sometimes to be a friend to yourself? I know sometimes, I'm afraid to speak up for myself because I want to be liked. Today, let's both work on speaking up for ourselves with courage and conviction, knowing that our friendship with ourselves is the basis for our friendship with others.

> *Be a friend to yourself, and others will be so, too.*
> — Thomas Fuller, Author

> *Our entire life, with our fine moral code and our precious freedom, consists ultimately in accepting ourselves as we are.*
> — Jean Anouilh, French Dramatist

Today, I'll be kind to myself and base my criteria for life improvements on acceptance of myself as I am.

HABITS FOR UNITY   Fuchsia

FEBRUARY 24
TODAY.... I remind myself - YOU COUNT

I read a quote that I can't remember exactly, but it was something like "Make memories today that you can live with tomorrow—and for the rest of your life." What profoundly good advice. Imagine how we all would behave each moment, if we really thought about the memories, we would be left with tomorrow.

> *Each of us is the accumulation of our memories.*
> — Alan Loy Mcginnis, The Romance Factor

> *The best thing you can give your children are good values, good memories and good food.*
> — Author Unknown

Today, I'll spend quality time with a child.

FEBRUARY 25

TODAY.... I remind myself - YOU COUNT

If we look at the BIG picture and realize that there is a place in it for each of us—then we have no choice but to be ourselves. If we were someone else, then there wouldn't be anyone to fill our place. You are the only person who can be you. If you decide to be another "them" instead of "you," your place will be left empty. Only you, being "you," can fill your place and your shoes.

> *Be yourself. Who else is better qualified?*
> — **Frank J. Giblin II, American Author**

> *We must be our own before we can be another's.*
> — **Ralph Waldo Emerson, American Author**

Today, I'll remind myself that I count with a bubble bath or a bouquet of flowers.

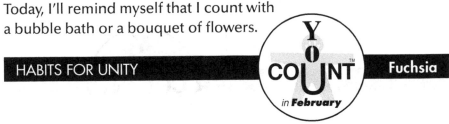

HABITS FOR UNITY   COUNT   Fuchsia
in February

FEBRUARY 26

TODAY.... I remind myself - YOU COUNT

Look for the signs people wear. Have you remembered to wear a little bit of the color "WOW Fuchsia" this month? Behind each person's words and deeds are signs that tell us who they are and what is important to them.

> *All children wear the sign: "I want to be important now." Many of our juvenile-delinquency problems arise because nobody read the sign.*
> — **Dan Pursuit**

> *To put yourself in another's place requires real imagination, but by so doing, each Girl Scout will be able to live among others happily.*
> — **Juliette Low, Founder, Girl Scouts**

Today, I'll be more aware of who others really are and of how they may view life from inside their hearts.

FEBRUARY 27
TODAY…. I remind myself - YOU COUNT

It is almost time to leave February. If there is one aspect of "You Count" that is most important, it is knowing that "you" make a difference with every single minute of the 1,440 minutes you have to spend each day.

> *Tomorrow is the most important thing in life. It comes into us at midnight very clean. It's perfect when it arrives and it puts itself in our hands. It hopes we've learned something from yesterday.*
> — **John Wayne, American Actor and Filmmaker**

> *You never get a second chance to make a first impression.*
> — **"Head and Shoulders" TV Commercial**

Today, I'll buy some colorful "WOW Fuchsia" balloons to celebrate me.

HABITS FOR UNITY   CO**U**NT™   Fuchsia
in February

FEBRUARY 28
TODAY…. I remind myself - YOU COUNT

You Count. A hopeful habit is a daily reminder that guides your actions toward making a positive difference, every minute, today and every day. Remember, this minute is only one of the 1,440 minutes you own today. How will your habits guide you to use the other 1,439?

> *You are a memory and a promise. I am a promise.*
> *I am a possibility.*
> — **Gloria and William Gaither, American Gospel Singers**

> *We're all in this leaky boat together.*
> — **Robert Oldenski**

Today, I'll commit to using my 1,400 POWER for good - every day of the year.

FEBRUARY 29

TODAY.... I remind myself, YOU COUNT

Every four years, I have an extra day for me. You have an extra day too. Together, let's use our extra day well. I'm glad that "I COUNT" but I'd love to count my life in 25% of the number of years by being born on February 29. Likely I would have hated being born on February 29 and having fewer birthdays when I was younger, but now, it would be so COOL to be much "younger." Either way, we all count.

We Count!

HABITS FOR UNITY | CO**U**NT | Fuchsia

March is Month 3

RESOLVE CONFLICTS

IN **MARCH**... and all year long...

Color Cue — Peaceful Dove Gray

Health Focus — Anger Management

Affirmation – TODAY, I strengthen my habit to
RESOLVE CONFLICTS

"Together we heal the country we all share."

– Elaine Parke

In MARCH, REMEMBER TO...
RESOLVE CONFLICTS

Last month, in February, we focused on our individual worth, personal empowerment, and on self-esteem. Individual efforts do quite a bit to change the world around us, but we can do so much more if we resolve conflicts and work together more often.

A dove has always been a symbol for peace so the color of peaceful dove gray is the celebration symbol for March's habit to Resolve Conflicts. Even if you began this month like a lion, decide to go out like a lamb. If losing your temper too quickly adds to the stress of conflicts with others, work on calming yourself down and taking time outs when you feel your emotional temperature rising.

The late advice columnist, Ann Landers, once suggested that we observe a National Reconciliation Day. As part of making this book work for you, you now have one whole month to do that—this month of March.

Resolving conflicts with someone that you disagree with takes a lot of courage, but this is the time to begin. Start with a smile and begin mending fences. Pick up the phone or write a letter. Take a few extra minutes with someone with whom you experience problems. Try to learn more about their point of view. Life is too short to hold grudges. Forgiving others is a great feeling. Reach out today, perhaps right in your own home. Lighten up, give a little and compromise. You will be happier and healthier for the effort.

Goal for the Month:
Patch-up a relationship with at least one person.

The Resolving Conflicts RAP

by Arnie McFarland, Written for March's habit in February 17, 1992

Sometimes there's a reason for the way you feel,
Cause somebody's made you mad.
     And there are times when someone is mad at you.
     Hey, you know that you've been bad.

Well, all of us know that for the month of March,
If we take the first step and try,
     To end the fight between them and you,
     You might get a big surprise.

If you forgive them and they forgive you,
You'll feel like a brand-new day.
     Resolving conflicts takes away stress.
     Come on! Try it the caring habits way.

In the month of March, it's "take the first step."
You know you can do it, too.
     Resolving conflicts isn't easy,
     But there's something in it for you.

Elaine Parke, guest speaking at a Rwandan Rotary Club in 2006, where, in memory of the genocide, they observed the 12 habits month to "Resolve Conflicts."

MARCH 1

TODAY... I strengthen my habit to RESOLVE CONFLICTS

Today, look for the lions of conflict and anger that are in your life now. Who are you on the "outs" with…? With whom are you not getting along? Where are the relationships that need resolution and healing before peace will come? Here is an excellent guideline:

> *When a person forgives another, he is promising to do three things about the intended wrongdoing:*
>
> *First: not to use it against the wrongdoer in the future;*
>
> *Second: not to talk about it to others; and*
>
> *Third: not to dwell on it himself.*
>   **—Jay Adams, American Author and Counselor**

Today: Walk away.

HABITS FOR UNITY   RESOLVE CONFLICTS *in March*   Dove Gray

MARCH 2

TODAY... I strengthen my habit to RESOLVE CONFLICTS

Peace is a key to happiness at every level—personally, in the family, in the community, in schools, in businesses, in America, and throughout the world. This month of March, "Let there be peace on earth and let it begin with me."

> *For it isn't enough to talk about peace. One must believe in it. And it isn't enough to believe in it. One must work at it.*
>   **— Eleanor Roosevelt, Former First Lady**
>
> *Violence is a one-way street to nowhere.*
>
> *— Author Unknown*

Today: Count to ten.

MARCH 3
TODAY... I strengthen my habit to RESOLVE CONFLICTS

There are people in our lives who are just plain "hard to get along with." A realistic solution in these situations is to let your problems with them roll off your back. Take a few minutes to chuckle at the humor of today's quote. However, in keeping with the spirit of *The Unity Habits*, I'm suggesting that you never think of another person as a pig.

> *Never get in a conflict with a pig. You'll both get muddy and the pig will enjoy it.*
> — **Cale Yarborough, American Auto Racer**

> *Laughter changes our perception of pain: physical and emotional.*
> — **Bob Basso, Ph.D., American Author and Speaker**

Today: Laugh.

HABITS FOR UNITY   RESOLVE CONFLICTS *in March* Dove Gray

MARCH 4
TODAY... I strengthen my habit to RESOLVE CONFLICTS

Have you ever met a person who builds up their own throne with bayonets? In daily life, one of the bayonets people use against each other is ridicule. Ridicule is a common tool of youth and adults who are bullies. Ridicule can be used to put people down. Do you know what it feels like when people ridicule you? How can you reduce the destructive use of ridicule in your own life today?

> *You can build a throne with bayonets;*
> *but you can't sit on it for long.*
> — **Boris Yeltsin, Former President of Russia**

Today: Love.

MARCH 5

TODAY... I strengthen my habit to RESOLVE CONFLICTS

We all know we don't like to be angry and that anger is stressful. It's easy to forget what anger does to us, while we're caught up in what we're doing to the other person. What we may not realize is that anger is self-destructive. It draws our mind and our energies away from meaningful tasks at work and at home. What does it take for you to let go of your anger and give yourself the freedom of a clear fresh mind?

> *Anger is a wind which blows out the lamp of the mind.*
> — **Robert Green Ingersoll, American Lawyer and Lecturer**

> *In your anger do not sin: Don't let the sun go down while you are still angry.*
> — **Ephesians 4:26-27.**

Today: Change your perspective on anger. It's not good for you.

HABITS FOR UNITY   RESOLVE CONFLICTS Dove Gray *in March*

MARCH 6

TODAY... I strengthen my habit to RESOLVE CONFLICTS

Forgiveness is a key to resolving conflicts because it is the part that we can control. We can NEVER control the other person—only ourselves. We can never change other people—we can only change ourselves.

> *If we feel we are wronged, we can't always get the other person to apologize, but we can be forgiving no matter what. A happy marriage is the union of two good forgivers.*
> — **Ruth Bell Graham, Wife of Billy Graham**

Today: Hold your breath for 10 seconds while you calm down.

MARCH 7
TODAY... I strengthen my habit to RESOLVE CONFLICTS

Sometimes, the best way to heal a small conflict is to simply change your own perspective. How big and how bad is the problem you're having with someone? Can you change your own perspective about it, rise above the problem, and go on as if there is nothing really wrong?

> *I just read that 1 out of every 4 people is unbalanced. Try to think of three of your best friends. If all 3 of your friends seem balanced and all right to you, then you must be the unbalanced one.*
> — **Slappy White, American Comedian**

Today: Close your eyes and picture a
beautiful scene—a beach or a
lush woodland.

HABITS FOR UNITY   RESOLVE CONFLICTS Dove Gray
in March

MARCH 8
TODAY... I strengthen my habit to RESOLVE CONFLICTS

"I need space." Have you ever said those words? Are you being truthful or stubborn? Are you fleeing from a problem with some-one instead of finding the courage to find a common ground of agreement? I have done both and find that escape is never a real solution, only a short-term gratification. Find a way to agree with someone; rise against the wind, even when it isn't easy.

> *"Birds in their little nests agree," he said. "So why can't we?"*
> — **John Steinbeck, American Author, The Winter of Our Discontent**

> *Don't be afraid of opposition. Remember, a kite rises against, not with the wind.*
> — **Hamilton Wright Mabie, American Essayist and Lecturer**

Today: Find a common ground.

MARCH 9

TODAY... I strengthen my habit to RESOLVE CONFLICTS

Getting in the middle of a problem between others is considered risky business. Maybe it's because our words may be perceived as fuel for their fire instead of a true interest in helping to solve the problem. Listen to a friend's complaints about another person with a true interest and intent to help them solve the problem. Work hard at not fueling their fire or adding to a chain of gossip.

> *My doctrine is this, that if we see cruelty or wrong that we have the power to stop, and do nothing, we make ourselves sharers in the guilt.*
>
> **— Anna Sewell, British Author, Black Beauty**

Today: Bake a cake for a friend
with a problem.

HABITS FOR UNITY   RESOLVE CONFLICTS Dove Gray
in March

MARCH 10

TODAY... I strengthen my habit to RESOLVE CONFLICTS

Successfully using humor in a "resolve conflict" situation is a matter of timing, but it can be done. When anger is high, humor can be interpreted as a belittling lack of respect for the other person's point of view. Begin to resolve a conflict by listening and negotiating. Use humor later in the process to bring emotions back together into a renewed common bond that humor can help to strengthen.

> *Using humor is like changing a diaper: it's not a permanent solution, but it makes everybody feel better.*
>
> **— Jeanne Robertson, American Comedian**

Today: Find humor in whatever the situation.
Humor is always there somewhere.

MARCH 11
TODAY... I strengthen my habit to RESOLVE CONFLICTS

I think love is the biggest and best four-letter word in the universe. There is nothing love can't face. There is no limit to love's faith, hope, and endurance. What do you think? Where can you give and receive more love in your own life?

> *What the world needs now is love, sweet love. It's the only thing that there's just too little of.*
> — **Hal David, American Composer**

> *Love cures people, the ones who receive love and the ones who give it, too.*
> — **Karl A. Menninger, American Psychiatrist**

Today: Spend time with someone you love.

HABITS FOR UNITY　　　　　　　　RESOLVE CONFLICTS　Dove Gray
in March

MARCH 12
TODAY... I strengthen my habit to RESOLVE CONFLICTS

Think about the words in your life that have broken your heart. Remember that angry words are often said as weapons rather than said as the truth. Today, let go of the hurts that angry words have caused you and feel the freedom. Make a commitment to yourself not to use those words in relationships with others.

> *Sticks and stones may break our bones,*
> *but words will break our hearts.*
> — **Robert Fulghum, American author and**
> **Unitarian Universalist Minister**

Today: Enjoy the beauty of a tree.

MARCH 13

TODAY... I strengthen my habit to RESOLVE CONFLICTS

Tolerance is a value that we all know is vital to living in peace with our neighbors. It's a puzzlement as to why we humans think other people have to be like us or think like us to be acceptable. We all know that life works because we are different and we each bring special gifts to life that enrich the world around us.

> *When we honor diversity, we have no enemies.*
> — **Jane Hughes Gignoux, American Author**

> *It is never too late to give up our prejudices.*
> — **Henry David Thoreau, American Author**

Today: Why don't trees get into fights?

HABITS FOR UNITY   Dove Gray

MARCH 14

TODAY... I strengthen my habit to RESOLVE CONFLICTS

Who wants to be wrong? I don't know anyone—do you? Today, think about someone you may not be getting along with right now. Is there some way that you can heal the relationship by taking more responsibility for what went wrong?

> *Two wrongs don't make a right, but two Wrights made an airplane*
> — **Anonymous**

> *Quarrels would not last long if the fault was only on one side.*
> — **Francois, Duc de la Rochefoucauld, French Prince and Author**

Today: Look into the other person's heart

MARCH 15
TODAY... I strengthen my habit to RESOLVE CONFLICTS

We've been strengthening our Habit to "Resolve Conflicts" for 2 weeks now. There is a process used by professional mediators to resolve conflicts that anyone can follow. There are some simplified versions available on the internet if you Google "mediation process." If you have a difficult conflict going on, perhaps you'll find some clues there to help you resolve it.

> *There is always hope when people are forced to listen to both sides; it is when they attend only to one that errors harden into prejudices.*
> — **John Stuart Mill, British philosopher**

Today: Commit to familiarizing yourself with the Meditation Process. You may never use all of the steps but knowing the process can help in other ways.

HABITS FOR UNITY   **RESOLVE CONFLICTS** Dove Gray
in March

MARCH 16
TODAY... I strengthen my habit to RESOLVE CONFLICTS

We live in such a complex and fast-paced world that even without a specific conflict with someone, it's easy to feel like we live in a battle zone. Our relationships can be part of our support system or part of our problems. What can you do today to be a support system for yourself and for others in your life?

> *There are enough targets to aim at without firing at each other.*
> — *Theodore Roosevelt, 26th President of the United States*

Today: Focus on the positives in your relationships and strengthen your support system by listening to and caring about others.

MARCH 17

TODAY... I strengthen my habit to RESOLVE CONFLICTS

Today is St. Patrick's Day. Conflict anywhere in the world is a choice.

> *Nothing is resolved by war. On the contrary, everything is placed in jeopardy by war.*
> — **Pope John Paul II, Address, Rome, 1992**

> *If we can't teach our children that fighting is not the answer, then we failed—as parents and as human beings. So, you can hit me, or you can shake my hand, the choice is yours.*
> — **Jason Seaver, "Growing Pains"**

> *Don't be a noble fighter, 'cause kindness is righter.*
> — **Popeye the Sailor Man, "The Popeye Cartoon Show"**

Today: Choose peace, not conflict

HABITS FOR UNITY   **RESOLVE CONFLICTS** *in March*   Dove Gray

MARCH 18

TODAY... I strengthen my habit to RESOLVE CONFLICTS

"Mend your fences" is an American idiom for the idea to "resolve conflicts." This has always puzzled me. Why would you repair a fence between yourself and someone else? The idiom says to keep your fences mended and strong instead of suggesting that you take them down. Think about any fences you may have in your life. Is it time to take them down?

> *Father Taylor of Boston used to say: 'There is just enough room in the world for all the people in it, but there is no room for the fences which separate them.'*
> — **Rita Snowden, New Zealander Author and Missionary**

Today: Contact someone and "mend" a relationship.

MARCH 19
TODAY... I strengthen my habit to RESOLVE CONFLICTS

Sometimes we can resolve conflicts by educating ourselves about the other person in the conflict. Have you ever experienced anger and irritation from someone, only to learn later that they were dealing with a terrible problem in their own life that had nothing to do with you?

> *There are only two ways of changing men (people)—one is by education of spirit, mind, and body, and the other is by violence. Education is the one peaceful technique for creating changes for the better.*
> — **Howard Haines Brinton, Quaker Author**

> *Let us convince our children that carrying a book is more rewarding than carrying a gun.*
> — **Author Unknown**

Today: Talk yourself out of anger

HABITS FOR UNITY   RESOLVE CONFLICTS Dove Gray
in March

MARCH 20
TODAY... I strengthen my habit to RESOLVE CONFLICTS

We can't spend this month strengthening our "resolving conflicts" habit without paying some attention to temper. In recent years, we have coined phrases like "road rage" to describe what happens when temper overtakes common sense that threatens even our physical safety behind the wheel of a car. Managing our own emotions takes courage and conviction. The easy way out is to blame the other person.

> *Hot heads and cold hearts never solved anything.*
> — **Rev. Billy Graham, American Evangelist**

> *Courage is the price life exacts for granting peace.*
> — **Amelia Earhart, American Aviatrix**

Today: While driving, listen to soft music. Think peace.

MARCH 21

TODAY… I strengthen my habit to RESOLVE CONFLICTS

I found more quotes about forgiveness than about any of the other concepts that help us resolve conflicts in our lives. Why is forgiveness so hard to do? Think about someone who you believe has wronged you today. What can you do to forgive them? Where do you need forgiveness?

> *Forgiveness is of the highest value, yet its cost is nothing.*
> — **Betty Smith, American Author, A Tree Grows in Brooklyn**

> *Life is an adventure in forgiveness.*
> — **Norman Cousins, American Political Journalist, World Peace Advocate**

Today: Forgive someone.
Forgive two people.

HABITS FOR UNITY   RESOLVE CONFLICTS Dove Gray   *in March*

MARCH 22

TODAY… I strengthen my habit to RESOLVE CONFLICTS

I chuckle at myself when I think about how perfect I'd be if I had never made the same mistake twice. Sometimes we get into conflict with ourselves because we expect so much and feel like a failure when we let ourselves down. Mistakes and wrong-doings are not to be taken lightly, but harboring guilt is never the way to improve yourself or to make your life better.

> *Experience enables you to recognize a mistake*
> *when you make it again.*
> — **Franklin P. Jones, British Publisher**

> *Forgive yourself. Then if you face a choice to be right*
> *or to be kind, choose kind.*
> — **Dr. Ernie Panza, Chiropractor and National Speaker**

Today: Forgive yourself.

MARCH 23
TODAY... I strengthen my habit to RESOLVE CONFLICTS

During the height of the peace movement in the 1960s, the Catholic Church had a great slogan, "If you want peace, work for justice." Sometimes we accuse our children unjustly when we don't know all the facts and react with our emotions instead of our hearts. Think about justice in your own life today. How can you be more caring and fairer in your judgment towards others?

Injustice anywhere is a threat to justice everywhere.
— **Martin Luther King, Jr., * Letter from Birmingham Jail, August, 1963**

Today: Intentionally be just and fair with others in your life.

HABITS FOR UNITY  Dove Gray

MARCH 24
TODAY... I strengthen my habit to RESOLVE CONFLICTS

Last month, we shared the idea that every day we have 1,440 minutes to spend for better or for worse. Life today is so filled with frustrations and complex problems that it would be easy to spend all of those 1,440 minutes being angry. This is where all those rages come from. Work on yourself to keep from getting caught up in it.

You can tell the size of a man by the size of the thing that makes him mad.
— **Adlai Stevenson II, American diplomat**

Nothing was ever gained by exchanging words in anger.
— **Gil Halswell, "Trackdown"**

Today: Belittle anger.

MARCH 25

TODAY... I strengthen my habit to RESOLVE CONFLICTS

The quote below about a hatchet handle really rings a bell with me. I'm one of those people who thinks I try to be forgiving. However, when I read this quote, I realized that I "leave a handle or two" sticking out for future use. How deeply do you bury hatchets in your life? Do you see any handles that need to be reburied?

> *Those who say they will forgive but can't forget – simply bury the hatchet, but leave the handle out for immediate use.*
> — **Dwight L. Moody, American Evangelist**

> *We pardon to the extent that we love.*
> — **Francois, Duc de la Rochefoucauld, French Prince and Author**

Today: Bury the hatchet and grind off the handle.

HABITS FOR UNITY   **RESOLVE CONFLICTS** *in March*   Dove Gray

MARCH 26

TODAY... I strengthen my habit to RESOLVE CONFLICTS

Think of a friend you know well. Then make a list of their faults. Then review the list to help yourself better understand why you see these qualities as faults. Could some of their faults be good attributes in certain circumstances? How sure are you about their faults? How important are their faults? Do they belong in your fault cemetery?

> *We should all keep a large cemetery in which to bury the faults of friends.*
> — **Ann Landers, Advice Columnist**

Today: Disagree with dignity – criticize the act, not the person.

MARCH 27

TODAY... I strengthen my habit to RESOLVE CONFLICTS

We have 1,440 minutes every day. If you were to plan how to use your minutes today, would you plan to use some for fighting, or in anger, or to hate? How can we be so illogical? How do we let ourselves become drawn into spending time so illogically?

> *Why hate when you could enjoy your time doing other things?*
> — **Miriam Makeba, South African Singer**

> *We must turn to each other and not on each other.*
> — **Rev. Jesse Jackson, American Civil Rights Activist**

Today: Plan your day well.

HABITS FOR UNITY   Dove Gray

MARCH 28

TODAY... I strengthen my habit to RESOLVE CONFLICTS

If we could resolve the issue of who is wrong and who is right in quarrels, there would be very few people fighting.

> *Quarrels would not last long if only one party were in the wrong.*
> — **Francois, Duc de la Rochefoucauld, French Prince and Author**

> *Come over to my side of the argument, the view is always so clear from here.*
> — **Ashleigh Brilliant, British Cartoonish**

Today: Do you care who is wrong and who is right?

MARCH 29

TODAY... I strengthen my habit to RESOLVE CONFLICTS

Attitude is a big factor in the resolution of conflict. Sometimes, we just have to be in an "open-hand" instead of a "clenched fist" frame of mind. Spend today being open minded and considerate of others.

> *You cannot shake hands with a clenched fist.*
> — **Indira Gandhi, Former Prime Minister of India**

Today: Open your hand and your heart.

HABITS FOR UNITY   **RESOLVE CONFLICTS** *in March*   Dove Gray

MARCH 30

TODAY... I strengthen my habit to RESOLVE CONFLICTS

Of all the quotes I collected for the month of March, this one by Mark Twain is one of my favorites. So often our Creator sends us examples through nature and this example of the violet is one to remember. This is a thought to take with you into April and all through the year.

> *Forgiveness is the fragrance the violet sheds on the heel that crushed it.*
> — **Mark Twain, American Author and Essayist**

> *Give and forgive.*
> — **Marie Teresa Rodet Geoffrin**

Today: Forgive someone - especially yourself.

MARCH 31

TODAY... I strengthen my habit to RESOLVE CONFLICTS

This is it—the 31st of March. Have you tied up your lions and brought lambs and white truce flags into your life? Have you treated yourself to the relief from stress that resolved conflicts can bring? You still have 1,440 minutes left in the month of March to "Resolve Conflicts." If there is more to do, then do it now. "Let there be peace on earth and let it begin with me."

> *When spider webs unite, they can tie up a lion.*
> — **Ethiopian Proverb**

Today: Leave your lions behind and hug a lamb today.

HABITS FOR UNITY  Dove Gray

April is Month 4

TAKE CARE OF OUR ENVIRONMENT

*IN **APRIL**... and all year long...*

Color Cue — Spring Green

Health Focus — Be Smoke-FREE!

Daily Affirmation – TODAY, I nourish my habit to
Take Care of Our Environment

"Together we heal the country we all share."

– Elaine Parke

In APRIL, REMEMBER TO...
TAKE CARE OF OUR ENVIRONMENT

It's APRIL—time to refresh and renew our interest in the outdoors. Think green... "Spring" Green. Pick a nice day and go outside, take a deep breath and smell the fresh spring breeze. Ahhhhhhhh...

That big breath of fresh air in our lungs is a good reminder to renew our commitment to the outdoor environment and to the future of the fragile planet we share. What we take care of today will be preserved for future generations. This is a time for us to appreciate and enjoy the beauty of the natural world.

> *The supreme reality of our time is the vulnerability of this, our planet.*
> — **John F. Kennedy, 35th President of the United States**

We know that our environment is made up of what we see, hear and breathe. What we often forget is that there is another climate that we live in—the climate of our relationships. Just for fun, here are a few silly jokes to boost your mood climate. They are only loosely connected to the environment but—so what?

Q. Where do baby cows eat?

A. In the Calf-eteria

Last night I had a dream that I was a tailpipe. I woke up exhausted.

Have a sunny breezy month. Think and wear spring green when you can. Take care of your environment.

Goal for the Month:
Select an environmental project as simple as planting a tree in your own yard.

Earth Pledge by Mac Gillis, Global Education Associates

I pledge allegiance to the earth
and all its sacred parts
Its water, land and living things,
And all its human hearts
I pledge allegiance to all life
And promise I shall care
To share and cherish all its gifts
with people everywhere.

Your Name _____

Date _____

In April – Take Care of Our Environment – Author enjoying one of nature's miracles by blowing dandelion fuzz with her grandson

APRIL 1

TODAY… I nourish my habit to
TAKE CARE OF OUR ENVIRONMENT

Today is April Fool's Day. Let's hope that we are not fooling our-selves into complacency about the threats to our sustainable envi-ronment. We are the caretakers of the earth for our children and for future generations. Together, we must all nourish the habit of earth stewardship.

> *We do not inherit the earth from our ancestors; we borrow it from our children.*
> — **Chief Seattle, Suquamish Chief**

Remember you are a very IMPORTANT part of the Earth. Care for it and be cared for by it.

HABITS FOR UNITY

Take Care of Our Environment *in April*

Green

APRIL 2

TODAY… I nourish my habit to
TAKE CARE OF OUR ENVIRONMENT

Let's take a second day to get ourselves in the "stewardship" frame of mind as we nourish our April habit. More than 35 years ago, John Kennedy recognized that saving our planet would take a global ef-fort, one person at a time. You and I are two people. We're already on our way.

> *The supreme reality of our time is the vulnerability of this, our planet.*
> — **John F. Kennedy, 35th President of the United States**

Love the Earth. Become the steward of a spot somewhere near home.

APRIL 3
TODAY... I nourish my habit to
TAKE CARE OF OUR ENVIRONMENT

Have you ever thought about how we relate to trees as symbols of steadfastness and continuity? We even invented "family trees" to represent family heritage and the future. Think about trees. Imagine yourself deep in a forest glade with the sun filtering down through the leaves. Do you have a favorite tree somewhere?

> *He plants trees to benefit another generation.*
> — **Caecilius Statius, Roman Comic Poet**

Protect our trees. Buy recycled paper products. Examine packaging to find the paper recycling emblem.

HABITS FOR UNITY   **Take Care of Our Environment** *in April*   Green

APRIL 4
TODAY... I nourish my habit to
TAKE CARE OF OUR ENVIRONMENT

> *Do Justice*
>
> *Learn from the world community*
>
> *Nurture People*
>
> *Cherish nature and the natural order*
>
> *Non-conform freely and ethically*
>
> *Live responsibly*
>   -- **Author Unknown**

Be proactive. Use your social media to inspire everyone you know to take care of their environment.

APRIL 5

TODAY... I nourish my habit to
TAKE CARE OF OUR ENVIRONMENT

Let's focus today on renewing our reverence and respect for the beauty of our environment and everything in it—especially for the beauty of one another. Close your eyes and think about the most beautiful place you know. Is it a building or is it a place in nature?

> *If you truly love nature, you will find beauty everywhere.*
> — **Vincent Van Gogh, Dutch Painter**

As you go through your day, really SEE what is around you.
Notice a tree, or a small animal or insect;
notice the delicacy of one simple
plant on a co-worker's desk.

HABITS FOR UNITY   **Take Care of Our Environment** *in April*   Green

APRIL 6

TODAY... I nourish my habit to
TAKE CARE OF OUR ENVIRONMENT

The following great quote by Walt Whitman really emphasizes the dilemma of our human condition and how uncomfortable it sometimes feels to be a person instead of a tree. Think like a tree today—firm, tall, knowing yourself, reaching for the heavens, and strong against the wind.

> *I like trees because they seem more comfortable with the way they have to live than other things do.*
> — **Walt Whitman, American Poet**

Go on a nature walk. Draw strength from the trees; notice their easily understood mission to guard their spot. Share their power, their steadfast refusal to be bowed down by the little day to day breezes that simply rustle their leaves and small branches.

APRIL 7

TODAY... I nourish my habit to
TAKE CARE OF OUR ENVIRONMENT

Contemplate and appreciate just one square inch of the ground at your feet.

> *The world cannot be discovered on a journey of miles, no matter how long, but only by a spiritual journey of one inch, very arduous and humbling and joyful, by which we arrive at the ground beneath our feet, and learn to be at home.*
> — **Wendell Berry, American Novelist/Environmental Activist**

Watch the journey of one bug for at least five minutes.

HABITS FOR UNITY  Green

APRIL 8

TODAY... I nourish my habit to
TAKE CARE OF OUR ENVIRONMENT

Our trees and forests are valuable to the future of our planet. Oxygen is critical to life itself. Trees breathe in our exhaled carbon dioxide and breathe out the life-giving oxygen we need to survive. That's only ONE of the reasons why our forests are so valuable to the future of our planet.

> *We must take action soon...for otherwise no forest— not even in the wildernesses of North America—will be safe in the future. If we continue this pollution at the present rate, there will be scarcely any trees left to worry about in a few decades.*
> — **John Seymour, Blueprint for a Green Planet**

Plant a tree.

APRIL 9

TODAY... I nourish my habit to
TAKE CARE OF OUR ENVIRONMENT

Look for joy in nature today. Whether we notice it or not, joy is abundant in everyday life. Unfortunately, we are often too busy and fail to notice it. Already today, a delicate little hummingbird came to the feeder outside my window. I will never cease to wonder at the beauty and the joyous energy of that tiny bird. Look for laughter, too. Laughter has been called a natural tonic for many of life's problems.

> *The earth laughs in flowers.*
> — **Ralph Waldo Emerson, American Poet**

Today, pick a small bouquet of flowers, or even just one blossom from your yard or an area where no harm would be done.
If this is not possible, then buy just one blossom at a florist and laugh in its beauty all day long.

HABITS FOR UNITY   **Take Care of Our Environment** *in April*   Green

APRIL 10

TODAY... I nourish my habit to
TAKE CARE OF OUR ENVIRONMENT

It may not be too soon to plant seeds or bulbs outside or you can start some inside in a pot or bowl. Some stores have bulb plants like tulips or hyacinths already planted and in bloom for immediate enjoyment. Think deliberately about the beauty of the flowers that will soon greet you. Think about it with anticipation and awe— imagine that a gift is on its way to you.

> *One of the healthiest ways to gamble is to bet on a spade and a package of garden seeds.*
> — **Dan Bennett, American Comedian**

Plant some seeds or bulbs today—set them on a sunny window ledge and anticipate.

APRIL 11
TODAY... I nourish my habit to
TAKE CARE OF OUR ENVIRONMENT

The best way to encourage taking care of our environment is to encourage all of us to care more for one another. A genuine concern for others helps us remember the person who may come by next, and might have seen the litter we could have thrown down ...
but didn't.

> *What the world needs now is love sweet love. It's the only thing that there's just too little of.*
> — **Hal David, American Composer**

Enjoy Keeping America Beautiful.
Make a list of parks to visit soon.

HABITS FOR UNITY  Green

APRIL 12
TODAY... I nourish my habit to
TAKE CARE OF OUR ENVIRONMENT

Once in a while it's a good idea to broaden our perspective by thinking about the big picture. When we feel stuck at home, remember we are always on a free trip around the sun.

> *Only nature does great things for nothing.*
> — **Anonymous**

> *Living on earth is expensive, but it includes a free trip around the sun.*
> — **Author Unknown**

Check out the scenery at no cost to you. Walk instead of using your car. Keep the scenery beautiful by putting litter where it belongs.

APRIL 13

TODAY... I nourish my habit to
TAKE CARE OF OUR ENVIRONMENT

I wonder if Cicero would have written the following quote if he were living down the street from you right now? Drinking in the beauty of flowers and appreciating nature is a human need that we too often miss out on. In the rush NOT to forget what we need from the grocery store like deodorant and sandwich bags, we let a great book lay unread and fail to look down at the flowers.

> *If you have a garden and a library, you have everything*
> *you need.*
> — **Marcus Tullius Cicero, Roman Statesman**

Fill your need to see beautiful flowers or read beautiful words today. Make your personal environment as uplifting as possible.

HABITS FOR UNITY   **Take Care of Our Environment** *in April*   **Green**

APRIL 14

TODAY... I nourish my habit to
TAKE CARE OF OUR ENVIRONMENT

> *We have available for human use, less than 1% of the total*
> *earth's supply of water. 97% is in our oceans and 2% is frozen.*
> — **Data from: The Water Pollution Control Federation**

> *How doth the little crocodile improve his shining tail? He pours*
> *the waters of the Nile on every golden scale!*
> — **Lewis Carroll, British Author and Poet**

Be a water leak detective and a pro-active water conservationist. Shorten your showers, aerate your faucets, put a displacement bag in your toilet tanks, and shorten the water flow when brushing teeth, washing dishes and shaving. Together we all can conserve our water for the years ahead.

APRIL 15
TODAY… I nourish my habit to
TAKE CARE OF OUR ENVIRONMENT

There is mounting evidence that having pets lengthens the quality and the duration of life for the sick and the elderly. We all have days when we feel like our pet is the only one who really cares about us. In the Old West, there were stories of mountain men like "Grizzly Adams" who preferred the company of animals to people.

> *Animals are such agreeable friends – they ask no questions;*
> *they pass no criticisms.*
> — **George Eliot, English Novelist**

Think about your pet or one that belongs to a friend.
Give a pet an extra hug or a rub down, or a treat. If you have an opportunity to help control the
pet population, do so.

| HABITS FOR UNITY | Take Care of Our Environment *in April* | Green |

APRIL 16
TODAY… I nourish my habit to
TAKE CARE OF OUR ENVIRONMENT

The color for this month is "Spring Green." Whenever you see or wear green, think of nature and of your responsibility for taking care of the land, the water and the living things around you. Be reminded to "celebrate nature," in all its glory. Have you ever been in the middle of a city with only cement all around you? How could we be happy without nature and beautiful living things?

> *Spring is Nature's way of saying, "Let's Party!"*
> — **Robin Williams, American Actor/Comedian**

Enjoy being outside. Be responsible when you are. Always cut plastic six-pack rings apart. They are not biodegradable and can choke or harm animals and marine life.

APRIL 17

TODAY... I nourish my habit to
TAKE CARE OF OUR ENVIRONMENT

Nature's perfection is filled with imperfections and no-one seems to mind. As a matter of fact, much of nature's beauty is formed by small disasters. We can take a lesson from nature when we think we have caused a "disaster" or even when we failed to do our best.

> *The woods would be very silent if no birds sang there except those who sang best.*
> — John James Audubon, Naturalist

> *A weed is but a modest flower*
> — Ella Wheeler Wilcox, The Weed

If you threw an aluminum can in the trash yesterday, you can do better today and this time, put one in the recycle bin.

HABITS FOR UNITY   **Take Care of Our Environment** *in April*   **Green**

APRIL 18

TODAY... I nourish my habit to
TAKE CARE OF OUR ENVIRONMENT

Helen Keller could neither see nor hear. Here is how she describes the story of her life. How can we not find joy and beauty in nature?

> *What a joy it is to feel the soft, springy earth under my feet once more, to follow grassy roads that lead to ferny brooks where I can bathe my fingers in a cataract of rippling notes, or to clamber over a stone wall into green fields that tumble and roll and climb in riotous gladness!*
> — Helen Keller, American Author/Activist

Close your eyes and enjoy nature with the rest of your senses.

APRIL 19

TODAY... I nourish my habit to
TAKE CARE OF OUR ENVIRONMENT

Share your growing reverence and sense of stewardship for our environment with children. Watch a nature program with them and talk about the message it held. Discuss what you are doing to protect our environment and why.

> *The supreme reality of our time is the vulnerability of this, our planet.*
> — John F. Kennedy, 35th President of the United States

Recruit children to learn the "other" 3-R's. Help them nourish their own habits to reduce, reuse and recycle. Encourage them to plant a tree for shade and oxygen.

HABITS FOR UNITY   Take Care of Our Environment *in April*   Green

APRIL 20

TODAY... I nourish my habit to
TAKE CARE OF OUR ENVIRONMENT

In America, we honor our Native Americans who taught us reverence for the land and for the Great Spirit who made it. Read some Native American poetry or books about the land. An interesting fact about the Cherokee hunting tradition is that warriors always kill the smaller weaker prey. This way the stronger of each species survives to reproduce.

> *Sell a country! Why not sell the air, the clouds and the great stream? as well as the earth? Did not the Great Spirit make them all for the use of His children?*
> — Chief Tecumseh, Shawnee Warrior

Tell a hunter what you now know about the Cherokee hunting tradition.

APRIL 21

TODAY... I nourish my habit to
TAKE CARE OF OUR ENVIRONMENT

This is Earth Day.

Celebrate EARTH DAY by wearing "Spring Green" and by saying the Earth Pledge. Re-dedicate yourself to doing your part to take care of and nourish our environment.

The Earth Pledge

> *I pledge allegiance to the earth*
> *and all its sacred parts*
> *Its water, land and living things,*
> *And all its human hearts*
> *I pledge allegiance to all life*
> *And promise I shall care*
> *To share and cherish all its gifts*
> *with people everywhere.*
> > **— Mac Gillis, Global**
> > **Education Associates**

| HABITS FOR UNITY |  | Green |

APRIL 22

TODAY... I nourish my habit to
TAKE CARE OF OUR ENVIRONMENT

TODAY, think about making an investment in our environment because it is something you value. What do you want to invest in? You can invest in the beauty of your own yard or a neighborhood park. You can contribute to an environmental organization or to a specific cause that saves forests or saves an endangered animal species. Whatever your choice, make an investment today.

> *The best investment on earth is earth.*
> > **— Louis Glickman, American Investor**

Help Save our Earth. Make your contribution today.

APRIL 23
TODAY... I nourish my habit to
TAKE CARE OF OUR ENVIRONMENT

Have you considered that the month to take care of our environment is a good time to quit smoking or to encourage someone else to do so? Scientists have proven the dangers of second-hand smoke. What better tribute to nature than to become SMOKE-FREE?

> *The garden of earth is the purest of human pleasures.*
> — **Francis Bacon, British Author**

Enjoy the human pleasure of nature by giving up the idea that smoking is a pleasure. Become a smoke-free advocate.
Stop or begin the process of stopping yourself from smoking.
Be an encourager to someone you know who
is trying to become smoke-free.

HABITS FOR UNITY   **Take Care of Our Environment** *in April*   **Green**

APRIL 24
TODAY... I nourish my habit to
TAKE CARE OF OUR ENVIRONMENT

People need nourishing, too. WE are part of the environment and we too can become withered and starved for affection and attention. Nourish the people around you. Look for ways to praise them.

> *I never saw a wild thing feeling sorry for itself.*
> — **D.H. Lawrence, English Poet/Writer**

Nourish other people by cleaning out your closets and basement to give a great load of clothing and other stuff to a thrift recycling store.

APRIL 25

TODAY... I nourish my habit to
TAKE CARE OF OUR ENVIRONMENT

April Rain Song

> *Let the rain kiss you.*
> *Let the rain beat upon your head*
> *with silver liquid drops.*
> *Let the rain sing you a lullaby.*
> *The rain makes still pools on the sidewalk.*
> *The rain makes running pools in the gutter.*
> *The rain plays a little sleep-song*
> *on our roof at night.*
> *And I love the rain.*

Water is precious; conserve it. Like the Amish, use a broom when it's raining and not a hose to clean your driveways, paths and steps. Save hundreds of gallons of water. Go ahead, put on that raincoat, or not, and let the warm rain cleanse your soul too. Then, sweep your driveway clean in the rain!

HABITS FOR UNITY | **Take Care of Our Environment** *in April* | Green

APRIL 26

TODAY... I nourish my habit to
TAKE CARE OF OUR ENVIRONMENT

We learn every day that our Earth is fragile—our atmosphere, our land, our water, and our delicate eco-cycle. Put yourself into nature and renew and refresh a love of the outdoors. Remember, the joy of nature's beauty is free.

> *Grasshoppers are*
> *Chirping in the sleeves*
> *Of a scarecrow.*
> — **Kawai Chigetsu-Ni**

Go on a nature walk and breathe the fresh air again. Ahhhhh... Also remember to turn off lights, stereos and TVs when you leave for your walk.

APRIL 27

TODAY... I nourish my habit to
TAKE CARE OF OUR ENVIRONMENT

EARTH SALUTE

> *I salute thee, O Earth, bearer of grain,*
> *Bearer of gold, of health, of clothes, of mankind,*
> *Bearer of fruit, of towers, generous, beautiful, unmoving,*
> *Patient, various, fragrant, fertile,*
> *Clad in a cloak all damasked with flowers,*
> *Braided with waters, motley with colors.*
> — **Guillaume de Salluste du Bartas, French Poet**

> *We must all cultivate our earth garden.*
> — **Voltaire, French Author**

Today, salute with joy and awe,
the earth and all of its treasures.

HABITS FOR UNITY   Green

APRIL 28

TODAY... I nourish my habit to
TAKE CARE OF OUR ENVIRONMENT

There is nothing lowly in the universe or in our neighborhood or
in our own household. You have 1,440 minutes each day to uplift
and take care of your family and your own household. This is where
stewardship begins.

> *Though I have looked everywhere, I can find nothing lowly in*
> *the universe.*
> — **A.R. Ammons, Still**

> *What we must decide is how we are valuable rather than how*
> *valuable we are.*
> — **Edgar Z. Friedenberg, American Author/Scholar**

Go to a favorite place in your own home and appreciate what you
have there. Clean it, dust it, sort through stuff; keep what you need
and pass what you don't onto others.

APRIL 29

TODAY… I nourish my habit to
TAKE CARE OF OUR ENVIRONMENT

Celebrate April every year by planting a tree. Place a "year planted" marker nearby. Take note of how much each tree is growing every year. Feel the pleasure of giving life to trees.

> *He who plants a tree plants a hope.*
> — **Lucy Larcom, American Teacher**

> *You can plant a dream.*
> — **Anonymous**

Save other trees by using sponges and cloth instead of paper towels and napkins. Use recycled paper at work.

HABITS FOR UNITY   **Take Care of Our Environment** *in April*   **Green**

APRIL 30

TODAY… I nourish my habit to
TAKE CARE OF OUR ENVIRONMENT

This is the last day of April. Hopefully, you have faithfully worked on nourishing your habit to take care of our environment. Remember that every day, the Earth calls us directly. If we listen, we allow her to keep on reminding us of her needs.

> *Mother Earth speaks boisterously with blazing flower hues and arrogantly with the dash of rustling willows. She glows in the bright green of a new spring leaf and caresses us with the feel of a water-worn stone. She embraces us with the fresh smell of a summer rain and touches our hearts through the brush of the evening breeze on our skin.*
> — **Author Unknown**

Have a sunny, breezy day, especially in your heart. As you leave the month of April, reflect on how well you have acquired the habit of stewardship for our environment. Thank you for all that you do and will do in the years ahead.

May is Month 5

BE GRATEFUL

IN **MAY**... and all year long...

Color Cue — Grateful Pink

Health Focus — Appreciate your body with Exercise.

Daily Affirmation – TODAY, I cherish my habit to
BE GRATEFUL

"Together we heal the country we all share."

– Elaine Parke

In MAY, REMEMBER TO...
BE GRATEFUL

"Be Grateful" is a perfect mental health Habit for May. During this special month we celebrate both Memorial Day and Mother's Day. Also, teachers, government service workers and many volunteers across America are honored and appreciated for all they do.

A great health tip for May is to show gratitude to your own body with some extra exercise. Experts tell us that exercise can make you feel happier because it produces changes in the parts of the brain that regulate stress and anxiety. At the very least, take more walks or take the stairs instead of elevators when you can.

Also, think pink this month. "Grateful Pink," is for Mom and for all those you appreciate everywhere. When I see or wear pink, I think "Grateful Pink" and of someone I can appreciate.

Even cool men wear pink. Pink is intuitive and insightful, showing tenderness and kindness with its empathy and sensitivity. Pink calms and reassures our emotional energies. Pink puts people in touch with the nurturing side of themselves.

Because I have been working on these 12 monthly habits for many years, I send many thank you notes during May. It has already become a "tradition" for me to do this. Maybe you can start your own "grateful" tradition. We have thirty-one days to work on being more grateful and appreciative.

Take time this month to celebrate "Be Grateful" in your own life and in your own way. Notice and appreciate workers you pass by on the street. Notice that person washing windows over there. How about telling them how nice they look as you pass by? Tell your children why you appreciate them. And don't forget to appreciate yourself. You are important too.

Goal for the Month:
In addition to appreciating others, take time to appreciate yourself — do something you've always wanted to do!

The Appreciation SNOWBALL

And.......Pass it on........

Be eager to do things asked of you.

Don't be "too busy."

See something that needs done.

Do it well without complaining or being asked to do it.

*Appreciate the earth - pick up litter, plant a tree or flowers –
Notice and appreciate the beauty of the world around you.*

*Put sunshine in someone's cloudy day with a kind word or a
sincere compliment.*

*Remember special days in May like Mothers' Day.............. treat it
SPECIAL!*

*Seek out elderly people and show that someone appreciates
them by sharing a hug, smile or a story.*

*Appreciate yourself - do something you've always wanted to -
count your blessings and your talents - how have you helped
others appreciate themselves.*

Appreciate the arts - go to a concert or a gallery.

Take stock daily - How have I shown appreciation today?

Offer to do each other's chores.

Trade shoes. Walk in someone else's shoes for a day.

*Select a special day for each person in your family.
Treat them royally.*

*Count blessings - fill a box with slips of paper with blessings
written on them. Share the blessing box when needed.*

*Penny jar - put a penny in for each act that shows appreciation.
Remove a penny for negative acts. Use all the pennies in the jar
for a class treat.*

*Select a new person each day and show them your appreciation,
mailman, teacher, friend.*

Make a personal list of things you appreciate in life.

*Add to it when you find new things you appreciate and refer to
it often to keep your positive attitude.*

— Mary McLeod Bethune, American Educator/Civil Rights Activist

Celebrating Being Grateful in May at the Morgan County Senior Center. The daily one-minute habit motivations were read daily and many activities and events featured the 12 habit themes.

MAY 1

TODAY...I cherish my habit to BE GRATEFUL

Today is MAY Day. This day has traditionally celebrated the coming of spring. In medieval England, May Day's main event was the Maypole Dance. Colorful dancers holding ribbons danced around the pole to welcome spring. Appreciating the beauty of nature in spring is a great note to start off May—the month to "Be Grateful."

> *Gratitude is the sign of noble souls.*
> — **Aesop, Greek Author/Philosopher**

This month, practicing praise and appreciation for others will help develop your own "attitude of gratitude." At the bottom of this month's daily habit motivationals, you'll find a "Praise Phrase" to practice as many times as you can during that day.

Praise Phrase # 1 — "You're great."

HABITS FOR UNITY   *Be Grateful in May*   Pink

MAY 2

TODAY...I cherish my habit to BE GRATEFUL

Life isn't perfect.

So often I catch myself falling into a state of feeling bad about what isn't the way I want it to be.

Thank you, Helen Keller, American Author (Blind) for these words:

> *"I thank God for my handicaps, for through them, I have found myself, my work, and my God."*

Praise Phrase # 2 — "You're very special."

MAY 3
TODAY...I cherish my habit to BE GRATEFUL

Keeping yourself in a grateful frame of mind is the best way to have a good day. Oprah Winfrey has found a way to increase our "attitude of gratitude" —the "Grateful Journal." This is a notebook (any notebook will do) that you keep near your bedside. She suggests that every night, you write down in the Journal at least five things that you are grateful for that day. Start a Grateful Journal and keep it going all month long.

> *Gratitude is the memory of the heart.*
> **— Jean-Baptiste Massieu, French Priest/Educator**

Praise Phrase # 3 — "Thank You."

HABITS FOR UNITY   Pink

Be
Grateful
in **May**

MAY 4
TODAY...I cherish my habit to BE GRATEFUL

During May, let's take time to show appreciation wherever we can. Make that pot of coffee for a busy spouse, or hug your child, or clean the kitchen or wipe the blackboard, or put paper in the copier at work. A great way to say "THANKS" is to "PAY IT FORWARD" when we can't return a favor.

> *The smallest good act is better than the most magnificent promises.*
> **— Anonymous**

> *He who received a benefit should never forget it; he who bestows one should never remember it.*
> **— Pierre Charron, French Philosopher**

P.S. And if, for a few minutes, there's no one around to appreciate, give a little to the sun, to the air and to a tree!

Praise Phrase # 4 — "You make a difference."

MAY 5

TODAY…I cherish my habit to BE GRATEFUL

While we're encouraging ourselves to praise and appreciate more, it's a good idea to think about the other end of the equation—being the recipient of praise.

> *Praise, if you don't swallow it, can't hurt you.*
> — **Mort Walker, Creator, "Beetle Bailey" Comic Strip**

> *Praise can be your most valuable weapon as long as you don't aim at yourself.*
> — **Orlando Aloysius Battista, Canadian-American Chemist/Author**

Praise Phrase # 5 — "I appreciate your humble attitude."

HABITS FOR UNITY | *Be Grateful in May* | **Pink**

MAY 6

TODAY…I cherish my habit to BE GRATEFUL

As children, we were taught to say "please" and "thank you" because it was good manners. What I've learned since then is that thankfulness is the path to fulfillment and a life full of joy.

> *Manners are the happy way of doing things.*
> — **Ralph Waldo Emerson, Poet, Author and Essayist**

> *A thankful heart is not only the greatest virtue, but the parent of all other virtues.*
> — **Marcus Tullius Cicero, Roman statesman**

> *Thankfulness is a sure index of spiritual health.*
> — **Dr. Maurice Dametz, Pastor/Physician**

Practice Praise Phrase # 6 — "I am thankful for you."

MAY 7
TODAY…I cherish my habit to BE GRATEFUL

Mother's Day is just around the corner. Mothers are real people in our own lives. The concept of mothering symbolizes the quality of cherishment for all living things; hence, "Mother Nature." Mothers aren't perfect, but they are yours. This month, take time to do more for your mom than send a card or make a quick phone call. Start by asking yourself, "What would Mom most like from me today?"

> *You only have one mom and you should appreciate her.*
> — **Sam, Age 12**

> *A company held a contest for kids with the theme: 'The Nicest Thing My Father Ever Did for Me.' One youth answered: 'He married my mother.'*
> — **Robert Sylvester, American Author**

Praise Phrase #7 — "Thanks Mom, you're the best."

| HABITS FOR UNITY | *Be Grateful in May* | Pink |

MAY 8
TODAY…I cherish my habit to BE GRATEFUL

If all of my good intentions were laid end to end… oh what long roads they would pave. I opened a drawer this morning and found an addressed "thank you" note that I had forgotten to send. What makes this month great is that we can use it to play "appreciation catch-up." It's never too late to say thank you.

> *The smallest good act is better than the most magnificent promises.*
> — **Thomas Babington Macaulay, British Historian**

> *A great way to say thanks is to pass it on when we can't return a favor.*
> — **Jeffrey A. Patrick, husband**

Praise Phrase #8 — "Thanks for showing me you care."

MAY 9

TODAY…I cherish my habit to BE GRATEFUL

Years ago, my son, Mike, went through a "negative attitude" phase, so I gave him a book called, The Praise Book. The point was that there is always something good you can say about everyone such as "you have great elbows," or "what a neat cupboard," or "you always have a nice smile." Try writing your own praise book this month with the things you say and do for others

> *When someone does something good, applaud!*
> *You will make two people happy.*
> — **Samuel Goldwyn, American Filmmaker**

> *Find the good and praise it.*
> — **Alex Haley, Author**

Praise Phrase # 9 — "Hooray for you."

HABITS FOR UNITY   *Be Grateful in May*   **Pink**

MAY 10

TODAY…I cherish my habit to BE GRATEFUL

"Counting your blessings" is a phrase everyone knows—but it is easy to forget when our favorite shirt comes out of the wash shrunken two sizes.

> *Blessings brighten while we count them.*
> — **Maltbie Davenport Babcock, American Clergyman and Writer**

> *Better to lose count while naming your blessings than to lose your blessings by counting your troubles.*
> — **Maltbie Davenport Babcock, American Clergyman and Writer**

Praise Phrase # 10 — *"I appreciate your work."
(*Be cautious if you're saying this to the person who shrunk your shirt.)

MAY 11
TODAY...I cherish my habit to BE GRATEFUL

Sometimes it does us good to appreciate the natural gifts that surround us—the air, the trees, the flowers and the sunshine or the rain. Sit quietly on a bench in the park or on a rock in the forest and look around you. Notice the gifts.

> *God took the time to create beauty, how can we be too busy to appreciate it?*
> — **Randall B. Corbin**

> *One touch of nature makes the whole world kin.*
> —**William Shakespeare, English playwright**

Praise Phrase #11 —
"You put a smile on my face."

HABITS FOR UNITY   *Be Grateful in May*   **Pink**

MAY 12
TODAY...I cherish my habit to BE GRATEFUL

Mary Poppins said, "A spoonful of sugar helps the medicine go down." There's also an old adage "you catch more flies with honey." Ben Franklin was credited with the quote, "Diplomacy is the art of letting someone else have your idea." It all adds up to the idea that giving respect and appreciation creates a two-way street that business people call the "win-win."

> *No One who achieves success does so without the help of others. The wise and confident acknowledge this help with gratitude.*
> —**Alfred North Whitehead, Mathematician and Philosopher**

> *Use soft words and hard arguments.*
> — **English Proverb**

Praise Phrase #12 — "You've got it now."

MAY 13

TODAY…I cherish my habit to BE GRATEFUL

One of the most difficult aspects of appreciation is expecting it. We know that we "shouldn't" expect anything in return when we give to others—but it is easier said than done. Building our habit of giving without expecting to be thanked is a good thing to work on this month.

> *Gratitude is a sometimes thing in this world. Just because you've been feeding them all winter, don't expect the birds to take it easy on your grass seed.*
> **— Bill Vaughan, American Columnist**

Praise Phrase # 13 — "You've earned a big hug for doing good without expecting gratitude."

HABITS FOR UNITY   Pink

Be Grateful in May

MAY 14

TODAY…I cherish my habit to BE GRATEFUL

Many things are said behind people's back that are harmful. Gossip is one of the worst in my book. Quiet gratitude in the form of a real "pat on the back" is one of the best ideas I've heard. Increasing your gratitude and praise vocabulary this month will bring benefits all year long.

> *The best thing to do behind a person's back is to pat it.*
> **— Franklin P. Jones, British Publisher**

> *Words of praise can heal relationships, resolve conflicts and improve your chances of professional success.*
> **— William F. O'Dell, American Author**

Praise Phrase # 14 — "I appreciate your directness."

MAY 15
TODAY...I cherish my habit to BE GRATEFUL

Manners are important. Once in a while, we can rely on manners to help us get through some tense moments. However, when manners come from the heart as well as from Amy Vanderbilt's Etiquette books, there is more caring and joy in the moment for all.

> *Gratitude is when memory is stored in the heart and not in the mind.*
> — **Lionel Hampton, American Band Leader**

> *The manner in which it is given is worth more than the gift.*
> — **Pierre Corneille, French Dramatist**

Praise Phrase #15 — "I appreciate your friendship."

HABITS FOR UNITY		Pink

MAY 16
TODAY...I cherish my habit to BE GRATEFUL

The "ILYAITYT" bedtime tradition began in our home more than 40 years ago. Today, it is still our special shorthand for the kind of love children need and want.

You can start the ILYAITYT tradition in your household this month. Make this secret code the last thought you share with your children just before they fall asleep every night. Oh yes, you'll need to know what it means. ILYAITYT stands for "I LOVE YOU AND I THINK YOU'RE TERRIFIC!

> *If you want your children to improve, let them overhear the nice things you say about them to others.*
> — **Haim Ginott, Child Psychologist**

Praise Phrase #16 — "ILYAITYT."

MAY 17

TODAY…I cherish my habit to BE GRATEFUL

I often wonder why business books and books about how to get along with people are on different shelves at the bookstore. Andrew Carnegie said that business success is 89% people skills and only 11% technical skills.

> *I have yet to find the man, however exalted his station, who did not do better work and put forth the greater effort under a spirit of approval than under a spirit of criticism.*
>
> **— Charles Schwab, American Financier**

> *Sandwich every piece of criticism between two layers of praise.*
>
> **— Mary Kay Ash, Cosmetics Founder**

> *People ask you for criticism, but they only want praise.*
>
> **— W. Somerset Maugham, British Author**

Praise Phrase # 17 — "Good job."

HABITS FOR UNITY  Pink

MAY 18

TODAY…I cherish my habit to BE GRATEFUL

Reinforcing the good qualities in children to build self-worth and self-esteem is invaluable to their future ability to succeed in life. Here are three quotes that together, say a volume of truths.

> *At the deepest place in human nature is the craving to be appreciated.*
> **— William James, American Philosopher**

> *It is not the mountain we conquer but ourselves*
> **—Sir Edmund Hillary, Explorer**

> *No one notices what I do until I don't do it.*
> **— Lorrie, Age 14**

Praise Phrase # 18 — "You mean the world to me."

MAY 19
TODAY...I cherish my habit to BE GRATEFUL

It's so great when once in a while we encounter positive surprises of kindness from strangers we will never see again. The "random acts of kindness" movement encourages this. When we can't repay a kindness, or even when we can, the best way to "Be Grateful" is to Pay it Forward.

Have you had a kindness shown? Pass it on.
— **Henry Burton, British Theologian**

Pay it forward with free compliments. They will be returned in due time.
—**David Chiles, Author of "Netiquette"**

Praise Phrase # 19 -- "Thanks for caring."

HABITS FOR UNITY	Pink

MAY 20
TODAY...I cherish my habit to BE GRATEFUL

I have read sad stories in books like "Chicken Soup" about people who failed to appreciate their loved ones and to tell them before losing them. You can write your own "happy ending" stories by remembering to be appreciative on a regular basis.

Please teach me to appreciate what I have before time forces me to appreciate what I had.
— **Susan L. Lenzkes, American Author**

Look at everything as though you were seeing it either for the first or last time. Then your time on earth will be filled with glory.
— **Betty Smith, American Author**

Praise Phrase # 20 — "I'm so glad you're in my life."

MAY 21

TODAY...I cherish my habit to BE GRATEFUL

I know there are days when life isn't going well, but everyone has great blessings in their lives. No one is an exception. On your darkest day, search around to find and remember the blessings in your life and your day will lighten.

It is not what we say about our blessings but how we use them that is the true measure of our thanksgiving.
— **W.T. Purkiser American, Preacher/Author**

Praise Phrase # 21 — "You can do it; you're on your way."

| HABITS FOR UNITY | **Be Grateful** in **May** | Pink |

MAY 22

TODAY...I cherish my habit to BE GRATEFUL

Because we have so many of them, it greatly improves our outlook to be grateful for the treasures of our normal days. Did you notice the beautiful child with her mother that you passed on the street today or the shape of a cloud in the sky?

Normal day, let me be aware of the treasure you are.
— **Mary Jean Irion, American Poet**

He who receives a benefit with gratitude repays the first installment on his debt.
— **Seneca Indian Saying**

Praise Phrase # 22 — "You're special."

MAY 23
TODAY...I cherish my habit to BE GRATEFUL

An anonymous quote I've heard many times is "I never saw a U-Haul truck in a funeral procession." It's humorous, but true— we don't really own anything but our hearts and our spirit. Even our bodies are rented for a certain length of time. From this "bottom line" perspective, think about "being grateful."

> *I don't have to have millions of dollars to be happy. All I need is to have some clothes on my back, eat a decent meal when I want to, and get a little loving when I feel like it. That's the bottom line, man.*
> — **Ray Charles, American Singer**

Praise Phrase # 23 — "I'm impressed."

HABITS FOR UNITY	Pink

MAY 24
TODAY...I cherish my habit to BE GRATEFUL

> *Gratitude makes sense of our past, brings peace for today and creates a vision for the future.*
> —**Melody Beattie, Author**

Legacy of the Teacher

> *I leave you love; I leave you hope.*
> *I leave you the challenge of developing confidence in one another.*
> *I leave you a thirst for education.*
> *I leave you respect for the use of power.*
> *I leave you faith.*
> *I leave you the dignity of your heritage and your future.*
> — **Jack Prelutsky, American Poet Laureate**

Praise Phrase # 24 — "I've got faith in you."

MAY 25

TODAY…I cherish my habit to BE GRATEFUL

Teacher Appreciation Week is in May. No matter what age we are, it's time to appreciate those special teachers in our lives. Take a moment this month, quietly, in your mind and heart, to remember and appreciate one special teacher. If you can reach them, let them know.

> *The class in school I hate the most is the one I learn the most from.*
> **— Joanne, Age 10**

> *Teachers are the best people in the whole world.*
> **— Natka, Age 14**

> *Sometimes a teacher who seems to be totally boring at the beginning of the year turns out to be the most awesome.*
> **— Robert, Age 12**

Praise Phrase # 25 —
"You're my teacher and my friend."

HABITS FOR UNITY   *Be Grateful in May*   **Pink**

MAY 26

TODAY…I cherish my habit to BE GRATEFUL

There is so much publicity about the problems kids have today and parents are being blamed for most of it. Let's start a rally this month to appreciate parents more and to criticize them less. After all, the best way to inspire anyone to improve is with praise and encouragement. Parents are no exception.

> *Parents don't get enough appreciation. If you want to make your parents feel good, write them a small note that says, "I love you."*
> **— Kim, Age 11**

> *Thanks an awful lot, Dad…it sure is good when your father's a friend.*
> **— Beaver Cleaver, "Leave It to Beaver"**

Praise Phrase # 26 — "I love you, Mom and Dad or Guardian."

MAY 27
TODAY...I cherish my habit to BE GRATEFUL

Appreciate yourself today. This one's for you. Have a month filled with joy and gratitude. Thank you for reading *The Habits of Unity*, One Month and One Citizen at a Time, and for choosing to learn to apply these life-changing habits to your own life.

> *Make the kind of memories that you want to live with forever.*
> — **Anonymous**

> *Were there no God we would be in this glorious world with grateful hearts and no one to thank.*
> — **Christina Rossetti, American Poet**

Praise Phrase #27 — "What would I ever do without you."

HABITS FOR UNITY  Pink

MAY 28
TODAY...I cherish my habit to BE GRATEFUL

In May we celebrate Memorial Day. It is a weekend of fun and picnics and enjoying the company of family and friends. During this weekend we will remember to quietly honor and praise those who served and those who died for the principles of the United States of America.

> *It is less appropriate to mourn the loss of valiant men who died than to thank God that such men lived.*
> — **George S. Patton, US General, World War II**

Praise Phrase #28 — "I honor you."

MAY 29

TODAY…I cherish my habit to BE GRATEFUL

Gratitude is rooted in the overall category of kindness and generosity. What's special about gratitude is that you can give it away for free, over and over again. You will make the recipients of your gratitude gifts just as happy as if you'd given them an expensive gift – just try it and see.

> *Kind hearts are the garden,*
> *Kind thoughts are the roots,*
> *Kind words are the blossoms,*
> *Kind deeds are the fruit.*
> — **John Ruskin, British Art Critic**

Praise Phrase # 29 — "Thank you for your kindness."

HABITS FOR UNITY   **Pink**

MAY 30

TODAY…I cherish my habit to BE GRATEFUL

If there is a universal language of appreciation, it is a smile. Try yours out in the mirror this morning. I'll bet you haven't seen it yourself for a while. Now try it out on everyone you meet today— they all try hard with their own lives and deserve appreciation too.

> *In all the countries I've been to, everyone understands and appreciates a smile.*
> — **Jennifer, Age 14**

> *Those who can receive bread and smile in gratitude can feed many without even realizing it.*
> — **Henri J.M. Nouwen, Dutch Theologian**

Praise Phrase # 30 — "What a great smile; you brighten my day."

MAY 31
TODAY...I cherish my habit to BE GRATEFUL

It's the end of May. I appreciate you. I appreciate that you have this book in your hand right now and are reading this. It means that we share a deep desire to make our own lives and the lives of those around us better. We can make a habit out of appreciating the fragile thread of life and treasuring the joy life brings.

We can be thankful for what we have or complain about what we do not have. One or the other becomes the habit pattern of our own life.
> — **Elisabeth Elliott, American Christian Author/Speaker**

Gratitude is the most exquisite form of courtesy.
> — **Jacques Maritain, French Philosopher**

Praise Phrase # 31 — "I appreciate you, the reader of this page

HABITS FOR UNITY   Be Grateful in **May**   Pink

June is Month 6

REACH HIGHER

*IN **JUNE**... and all year long...*

Color Cue — "JOLT" Orange

Health Focus — Improve Your Health with Prevention

Daily Affirmation – TODAY, I discover my habit to
REACH HIGHER

"Together we heal the country we all share."

– Elaine Parke

In JUNE, REMEMBER TO...
REACH HIGHER

I WILL DREAM. I WILL BE ADVENTUROUS.
I WILL IMPROVE MYSELF.

This month's celebration color is "JOLT Orange." It cries out to be different. Use it as your secret reminder to encourage yourself and to have faith that you will accomplish your goals. Know that you CAN do it—whatever it is.

Let June's daily messages inspire and uplift you and set you free from the boundaries around you. Of all of the twelve Habits, this month's "Reach Higher" needs to be inspired to be achieved. We are able to bloom and grow in direct proportion to our willingness to dream.

While working on "*The Habits of Unity*" ... one month and one person at a time, I've read through thousands of quotes trying to find just the right ones to help each of us become our own "better selves" more often. Here is a quote to start off June. It is one of my favorites. It makes me laugh and cry at the same time.

> *Millions long for immortality who don't know what to do on a rainy afternoon.*
> — **Susan Ertz, British American Author**

Goal for the month:
Break free of procrastination. Do the important task that you have been putting off for too long.

Dreams

> *Hold fast to dreams*
> *for if dreams die*
> *Life is a broken winged bird*
> *That cannot fly.*
>
> — **Langston Hughes, American Poet/Social Activist**

I have learned a deep respect for one of Goethe's couplets:

"Whatever you can do, or dream you can, begin it.
Boldness has genius, power, and magic in it!"

Until one is committed, there is hesitancy, the chance to draw
back, always ineffectiveness. Concerning all acts of initiative (and
creation), there is one elementary truth, the ignorance of which
kills countless ideas and splendid plans: that the moment one
definitely commits oneself, then Providence moves too.

All sorts of things occur to help one that would never
otherwise have occurred. A whole stream of events issues
from the decision, raising in one's favour all manner of
unforeseen incidents and meetings and material assistance,
which no man could have dreamt would have come his way.

— **William Hutchison Murray, Scottish Writer**

Song for John

On a windy day let's go flying
There may be no trees to rest on
There may be no clouds to ride
But we'll have our wings and the wind will be with us
That's enough for me, that's enough for me.

— **Yoko Ono, Widow of John Lennon**

June's Caring Habit to "Be Adventurous" and to "Reach Higher" – being used to inspire young people in Berkeley Springs, WV to stay away from drugs at a "Don't Use Drugs" festival. The color is "Jolt Orange." Volunteers, Lori Michael and Norene Brown are manning the booth.

This is Danny Rhodes, a 12 Habits Community Materials Delivery Ambassador during June's month to "Reach Higher" and look for your possibilities. Students and community members could take "Possibilities Gold Coins" to remember to "Reach Higher."

JUNE 1

TODAY... I discover my habit to REACH HIGHER!

Take an extra moment to re-inspire your daily journey through June by rereading and reflecting on the two poems at the beginning of the chapter. Read them every day. Feel your heart uplifted and guided toward your dreams. Of all the twelve Habits, "Reach HIGHER" needs you to have faith in yourself and sometimes even courage. Growth only happens when there are dreams gliding on your wings of joy.

> *Growth is the only evidence of life.*
> **— John Henry Cardinal Newman, British Theologian**

> *On this narrow planet, we have only the choice between two unknown worlds.*
> **— Colette, French Author**

Today, choose new life, confidence, love, joy, faith, hope.

| HABITS FOR UNITY | REACH HIGHER *in June* | Orange |

JUNE 2

TODAY... I discover my habit to REACH HIGHER!

Nobody ever said life is easy. So often, we postpone our dreams until "things smooth out" or until our problems disappear or we have more time. Dreams will never happen in our lives unless we start toward them now. Tough times are often the most fertile ground for converting problems into opportunities we never believed would come our way.

> *When the going gets tough, the tough get going.*
> **— Joseph P. Kennedy, Businessman**

> *If there is no struggle there is no progress.*
> **— Frederick Douglass, American Social Reformer**

Wear orange or an orange accessory—notice orange today.

JUNE 3
TODAY... I discover my habit to REACH HIGHER!

A dream happens all in one night, but our living hopes and dreams never materialize that quickly. Whatever your self-improvement goals are this month—they will happen in a series of many single steps—some firm, some faltering and some wrong—that must be redirected. I call this series of steps toward dreams ``the bread crumb path." What will you call the path you walk?

> *According to the ancient Chinese proverb: 'A journey of a thousand miles must begin with a single step.'*
> — **John F. Kennedy, 35th President of the US**

> *Mountain, get out of my way.*
> — **Montel Williams, Talk-Show Host**

Eat just one potato chip;
then put the bag away.

HABITS FOR UNITY   Pink

JUNE 4
TODAY... I discover my habit to REACH HIGHER!

It's so easy to keep life just the way it is. Is this daily schedule familiar?

6:00 am	Alarm rings
6:15 am	Alarm rings again
6:30 am	Hit the shower
7:00 am	Feed kids and get them off to school
8:00 am	Leave for work
9:00 - 12:00 pm	WORK
12:00 - 1:00 pm	Lunch
1:00 - 5:00 pm	WORK
6:00 pm	Dinner
8:00 pm - ?	Put kids to bed
10:00 pm - ?	Fall asleep while watching TV

Tuck something special, like a little note, into a lunch box, briefcase, pocket or purse.

JUNE 5

TODAY... I discover my habit to REACH HIGHER!

Make at least one difficult decision today. Choose the one you have been putting off the longest. Getting past that decision and finally moving forward will release your mind and emotions to fly free towards a happier day.

> *The difficulty in life is the choice.*
> — **George Moore, "The Bending of the Bough"**

> *We cannot become what we need to be by remaining what we are.*
> — **Max De Pere, Leadership Is an Art**

Draw a map of your journey.
Mark the difficult decisions with
an erasable marker.

HABITS FOR UNITY   REACH HIGHER *in June*   Orange

JUNE 6

TODAY... I discover my habit to REACH HIGHER!

Most choices involve going toward or away from something or someone. Think about your choices today—what loss are you risking by taking a step toward your goals? Is fear and the risk of loss holding you back? What is your "second base?" Take one step to get there.

> *Progress always involves risk; you can't steal second base and keep your foot on first.*
> — **Frederick Wilcox, British Footballer**

> *I don't want the cheese; I just want to get out of the trap.*
> — **Spanish Proverb**

> *Why not go out on a limb? Isn't that where the fruit is?*
> — **Frank Scully, American Journalist**

Find a tree and climb it. Look at life from a higher perspective.

JUNE 7
TODAY… I discover my habit to REACH HIGHER!

Considered how impossible human flight must have seemed before the first flight on December 17, 1903? Wilber and Orville Wright overcame the impossibility of human flight by building a plane that flew. What do you believe is impossible in your life? Write an action plan and timetable to accomplish your own "Impossible."

> *I have learned to use the word impossible with the greatest caution.*
> — **Wernher von Braun, German Rocket Scientist**

> *Determine that the thing can and shall be done, and then we shall find the way.*
> — **Abraham Lincoln, 16th President of the US**

Watch and wait for the first star to appear in the evening sky. That star is your star.

HABITS FOR UNITY   Orange

JUNE 8
TODAY… I discover my habit to REACH HIGHER!

The first step is the hardest. The first step contains a fear of the unknown that we only have to overcome once in order to move ahead. This seems simple enough, but we know from experience that it is not. Think about the times you took the first step to resolve an argument. Do you remember the fear? After the argument was resolved, do you remember the joy and the relief of regaining a friendship that was in danger of being lost?

> *You miss 100% of the shots you never take.*
> — **Wayne Gretzky, Canadian Hockey Player**

> *Either move or be moved!*
> — **Colin Powell, Retired General United States Army**

Forgive someone whom you thought you couldn't forgive. Do it today.

JUNE 9
TODAY... I discover my habit to REACH HIGHER!

Because you are reading this book, you are not one of America's illiterate adults. Let the courage of those adults who have entered literacy programs and done the work to learn to read inspire you to do more reading. Read to a child whenever you can. You are one of the lucky ones.

> *To delight in reading is to trade life's dreamy moments for moments of pure joy.*
> — **Charles De Secondat, Baron de Montesquieu**

> *Books are keys to wisdom's treasure;*
> *Books are gates to lands of pleasure;*
> *Books are paths that upward lead;*
> *Books are friends. Come, let us read.*
> — **Emilie Poulsson, American Children's Author**

Volunteer in an adult literacy program or read to a child.

HABITS FOR UNITY   REACH HIGHER™   *in June*   Orange

JUNE 10

TODAY... I discover my habit to REACH HIGHER!

Boldness doesn't have to be loud and pushy. Boldness is the quiet first step of courage...the step that is most difficult to take. The following quote by the German poet, Johann Goethe is one of my all-time favorites. It inspired me to leave my "cushy" job in corporate America and bring to life my dream that the 12 Habits of "*The Habits of Unity*" can encourage all of us toward a more unified and compassionate society.

> *Whatever you can do or dream you can begin it. Boldness has genius, power and magic in it.*
> — **Johann Goethe, German Poet**

Sit outside and dream. Who are you? What are your gifts? What is your calling?

JUNE 11
TODAY... I discover my habit to REACH HIGHER!

Thomas Edison tried nearly 1,000 ways to make a light bulb before he found the way that worked. Thank God, he did NOT have an instruction book. He knew that while discoveries are partly inspiration, they are mostly perspiration.

> *Discoveries are often made by not following instructions, by going off the main road, by trying the untried.*
> — **Frank Tyger, American Editorial Cartoonist**

> *Trials are trails to higher ground.*
> — **S. Samuel Venechanos, American Poet**

Find a nearby park with walking trails.
Choose a path you have never taken.

| HABITS FOR UNITY | REACH HIGHER *in June* | Orange |

JUNE 12
TODAY... I discover my habit to REACH HIGHER!

Vision and wonder go hand in hand. There is a sacred quality to wonder. Life is sweet when we remain childlike with a capacity for wonder and awe. Too often we think that being a grown-up means leaving childlike wonder behind.

> *Life is the childhood of our immortality.*
> — **Johann Goethe, German Poet**

> *The world will never starve for wonders, but only for want of wonder.*
> — **G.K. Chesterton, British Author**

> *Vision is the art of seeing things invisible.*
> — **Jonathan Swift, British Author**

Observe with wonder, a flower, an insect, a bird, a child.

JUNE 13

TODAY... I discover my habit to REACH HIGHER!

Curiosity is a first cousin to wonder and vision. I think curiosity is the spice of life. What fun it is to make a discovery, even a small one. What discovery did you make yesterday? Perhaps you discovered many new things.

> *Be curious always! For knowledge will not acquire you; you must acquire it.*
> — **Sudie Back, Author**

> *Nothing is interesting if you're not interested.*
> — **Helen MacInnes, Scottish-American Author**

Learn something new. Look it up in an encyclopedia or find it on the internet. Perhaps learning to use the internet is a challenge you want to conquer this month.

HABITS FOR UNITY   **REACH HIGHER** *in June*   Orange

JUNE 14

TODAY... I discover my habit to REACH HIGHER!

Today is Flag Day. It's the date in 1777 when Americans adopted our flag.

> *In America, getting on in the world means getting out of the world we have known before.*
> — **Ellery Sedgwick, American Editor**

> *In America, nobody says you have to keep the circumstances somebody else created for you.*
> — **Amy Tan, Japanese-American Author**

What does America mean to you? If you don't have a flag, buy one. Hang it today.

JUNE 15
TODAY... I discover my habit to REACH HIGHER!

It's halfway through June. Here are some quick and easy
"Reach Higher" ideas:

> Read a book to your child.
> Ride a bike trail.
> Visit a historical site.
> Learn to play a new sport.
> Practice a random act of kindness.
> Plan a vacation.
> Plan a "date" with your spouse.
> Volunteer to work a few hours for a local charity.
> Get tickets to attend a local play.
> Send a "thinking of you" card to someone.
> Plan an activity for a group you work with.

Smile, smile, smile.

HABITS FOR UNITY   **REACH HIGHER** *in June*   Orange

JUNE 16
TODAY... I discover my habit to REACH HIGHER!

When we're stuck and can't get over a hurdle, the view remains
the same unless we go forward. What kind of fears and worries are
keeping you down? What can you do to continue the joy and the
journey of life?

> *Stop worrying about the potholes in the road and celebrate
> the journey.*
> — **Fitzhugh Mullan, M.D. and Barbara Hoffman, Authors**

> *A man's reach should exceed his grasp, or else what is heaven for?*
> — **Robert Browning, British Poet**

> *The only thing worse than failing is being afraid to try.*
> — **Frank Mingo**

Next time you're driving, go ahead—hit a pothole. Just a very little
one. I don't want to be responsible for ruining your car.

JUNE 17

TODAY... I discover my habit to REACH HIGHER!

Focusing on self-improvement wouldn't be complete without the topic of education. How many people are limited by not having the education they need? What have you been putting off? Is your dream to learn a career or to re-educate yourself for a new career? Would you like to learn to skydive, or to play an instrument? This month, June, it's time to spread your wings and fly!!!

Education's purpose is to replace an empty mind with an open one.
— Malcolm S. Forbes, American Businessman

Where there is an open mind, there will always be a frontier.
— Charles F. Kettering, American Engineer

Find one educational source locally or on-line. Sign up to take a course.

HABITS FOR UNITY   Orange

JUNE 18

TODAY... I discover my habit to REACH HIGHER!

One of the best ways to stay in a rut is to procrastinate. Close your eyes for a minute and think about the issues in your own life. Where do you feel stress? Is the stress coming from something you should be doing and don't? Here's a couple of quotes with a little humor to speed your actions along:

When you wait, all that happens is that you get older.
— Larry McMurtry, American Author

If opportunity doesn't knock—build a door.
— Milton Berle, American Comedian

Use five free minutes to start building the door to a new project.

JUNE 19
TODAY... I discover my habit to REACH HIGHER!

This month we celebrate Father's Day. I read the quote below about growing up and laughed because it describes parenting as well as childhood. So few of us have ever taken parenting courses. We parent with "how?" instead of "know-how." We lead with our hearts and hope our "series of advances" produce healthy, well-adjusted children. Of all life's roles, parenting is one that is the most challenging.

We honor and appreciate you, DAD. It's a difficult job.

> *Growing up doesn't have to be so much a straight line as a series of advances.*
> **— Kevin Arnold, "The Wonder Years"**

> *Life is at its best when it's shaken and stirred.*
> **— F. Paul Faculte**

Send cards or greetings to your favorite father(s) or father figures.

HABITS FOR UNITY   **R**EACH **H**IGHER™ *in June*   **Orange**

JUNE 20
TODAY... I discover my habit to REACH HIGHER!

I found the following two quotes and discovered that they go together. If we just turn stumbling blocks into stepping stones and then lay them across the river that looks a hundred miles wide, we will reach our dreams on the other side—OF COURSE. It will be easy.

> *...That river looks a hundred miles wide - when all your dreams are on the other side.*
> **— Barry Manilow, American Singer**

> *One of the secrets of life is to make stepping stones out of stumbling blocks.*
> **— Jack Penn. American Author/Surgeon**

When it rains, watch the individual raindrops fall—think of oceans.

JUNE 21

TODAY... I discover my habit to REACH HIGHER!

Look ahead to the joyous journey of a new day. Today, you have 1,440 minutes to shine and to make a difference. If you want to look back now and then, look back to the month of May. Remember to be appreciative and thankful for each tiny moment we have each day.

> *Don't look back. Something may be gaining on you.*
> — **Satchel (Leroy) Paige, American Baseball Player**

Take an extra moment of preparation to look your best in honor of the new day.

HABITS FOR UNITY   **R**EACH **H**IGHER *in June*   Orange

JUNE 22

TODAY... I discover my habit to REACH HIGHER!

Everything man-made is created from the thoughts and dreams of someone. Every building, every light bulb, every popsicle stick, every box of chocolate cake mix, every paper clip, every clock, every jelly bean, and every hula hoop began as a dream of possibility in the mind of one person.

> *It is said that a man's life can be measured by the dreams he fulfills.*
> — **Mr. Roarke, "Fantasy Island"**

> *Don't wait for your ship to come in. Swim out to it.*
> — **Anonymous**

> *I like the dreams of the future better than the history of the past.*
> — **Thomas Jefferson, Third President of the US**

Make room in your life to begin your dream(s).

JUNE 23
TODAY... I discover my habit to REACH HIGHER!

Be Adventurous! Take today off.

"Forget" to open your emails and messages today.
They can wait!

HABITS FOR UNITY   **R**EACH **H**IGHER in **June**   Orange

JUNE 24
TODAY... I discover my habit to REACH HIGHER!

There have always been great explorers among us. Perhaps it's because there's fascination in the act of thrusting forward and traveling to new places or making new discoveries. Sometimes, the challenge is just going through a door simply because you find it in front of you. You have no idea what is on the other side, but you are willing to take the risk to find out.

> *I think that man loses something if he has the option to go to the moon and does not take it.*
> — **Neil Armstrong, American Astronaut**

If you haven't already done it, learn how to get on the internet. If you have already mastered that, learn something new about the internet.

JUNE 25

TODAY... I discover my habit to REACH HIGHER!

The following quote is beautiful and completes our inspiration for the day. If it's too late for the sunrise, then watch the sunset. Watch the sun go all the way down until you can't see it anymore. Be adventurous. Just do it.

> *Climb up on a hill at sunrise. Everybody needs perspective once in a while, and you'll find it there.*
> — **Robb Sagendorph, Publisher, Farmer's Almanac**

Watch a sunrise or a sunset today.

HABITS FOR UNITY   Pink

JUNE 26

TODAY... I discover my habit to REACH HIGHER!

We're working on building our courage to follow dreams this month. Today, the question is: Are there other people in your life with dreams? How can you help them achieve their dreams? Each day, we are an instrumental part of the dream-building process for our children. Through us, they learn to reach higher or not.

> *As we make it, we've got to reach back and pull up those left behind.*
> — **Joshua I. Smith, Maxima Corp. Founder**

Help a child with a problem or help someone solve a dilemma they are facing.

JUNE 27
TODAY... I discover my habit to REACH HIGHER!

Dreams are the stuff that life is made of. Read again, the Langston Hughes poem that is at the beginning of the chapter.

> *Everything starts as somebody's daydream.*
> — **Larry Niven, American Author**

> *Dreams are necessary to life.*
> — **Anais Nin, French-American Essayist**

> *A world without dreams and hopes is no world at all.*
> — **Aretha Franklin, American Singer**

> *The wild dreams of today are the practical realities of tomorrow.*
> — **Captain Crane, "Voyage to the Bottom of the Sea"**

Dream of being different; serve a backwards meal, starting with dessert.

HABITS FOR UNITY   REACH HIGHER *in June*   Orange

JUNE 28
TODAY... I discover my habit to REACH HIGHER!

Make total health a "reach higher" goal for yourself and your family.

> *The key to exercising a family is not to get the kids to work out like adults, it's to get the parents to play like the kids.*
> — **Anonymous**
> *Weight loss doesn't begin in the gym with a dumbbell; it starts in your head with a decision.*
> — **Toni Sorenson**

> *Parsley is a decoration that diverts your attention from the small size of the entrée.*
> — **Elaine Parke**

Serve dinner on a teacup saucer.
Eat VERY slowly. Enjoy each bite.

JUNE 29

TODAY... I discover my habit to REACH HIGHER!

Hopefully this month, you've opened your eyes to some new possibilities in your life. I hope you've discovered the joy of breaking new ground and of getting unstuck from attitudes or actions that haven't brought you the happiness you deserve.

> *If a window of opportunity appears, don't pull down the shade.*
> — **Tom Peters, American Author**

> *We are born with our eyes closed and our mouths open, and we spend our whole lives trying to reverse that mistake of nature.*
> — **Dale E. Turner, American Actor**

When driving home today, take a wrong turn to see what's down that road.

HABITS FOR UNITY   REACH HIGHER *in June*   Orange

JUNE 30

TODAY... I discover my habit to REACH HIGHER!

Today is the last day of June. It's finally time to bring up the ghastly idea of defeat and quitting. Today is NOT the day to quit Reaching Higher. Today is the day to recommit yourself to all the great projects or promises you made to yourself to achieve your dreams. You might even promise yourself to get started on a few more.

> *Being defeated is often a temporary condition.*
> *Giving up is what makes it permanent.*
> —**Marilyn vos Savant, Magazine columnist**

> *You're never a loser until you quit trying.*
> —**Mike Ditka, Football player and coach**

If at first you don't succeed try again and again, but above all, never quit.

July is Month 7

BECOME INVOLVED

*IN **JULY**... and all year long...*

Color Cue — Patriot Red

Health Focus — Hygiene and Cleanliness

Daily Affirmation – TODAY, I honor my habit to
BECOME INVOLVED

"Together we heal the country we all share"

– Elaine Parke

In JULY, I REMEMBER TO...
BECOME INVOLVED!!

"Become Involved" is what America's founding fathers did when they knew they could create a better life for the early colonists. Because our founders were revolting against their loss of rights under Britain's rule, they created a Bill of Rights along with the Constitution. What they failed to do is to balance those rights with a list of responsibilities for all of us to practice to be good citizens in our democracy. Good citizenship is more than just voting. July is a great month to give meaning to your 4th of July Celebration by volunteering your time to a cause that is important to you. "Patriot Red" is just the color to encourage you to do it!

Red signifies a pioneering, patriotic spirit and leadership qualities, promoting ambition and determination. It is also a warm and positive color associated with our most physical needs and our will to survive. Because the dangerous COVID virus is still ever-present, the health benefits of cleanliness and hygiene have become even more important.

Here's a place to make your own personal plan for Becoming Involved.

MY PERSONAL "BECOME INVOLVED" PLAN

GOALS: _____

_____

_____

_____

PLAN OF ACTION: _____

_____

_____

_____

Goal for the month:
Have a great summer by volunteering at least some of your time

The Ripple Effect

Drop a stone into the water
    In a moment it is gone,
Yet there are a hundred ripples
    Circling on and on.

Say an unkind word this moment,
    In a moment it is gone,
Yet there are a hundred ripples
    Circling on and on.

Say a word of cheer and splendor
    In a moment it is gone,
Yet there are a hundred ripples
    Circling on and on.

— Anonymous

JULY 1

TODAY... I honor my habit to BECOME INVOLVED

July is flavored with love of America, our country. It is a month of family and neighborhood gatherings. Patriot Red is the color of nationalism. It's a good time to think about your community and to consider your own role in it. Organizations and ideas for volunteering will be shared with you each day this month. People who become involved make a caring difference.

> *If we do not lay out ourselves in the service of mankind whom should we serve?*
> — **Abigail Adams, Former First Lady**

> *In a world where there is so much to be done, I feel strongly impressed that there must be something for me to do.*
> — **Dorothea Dix**

Volunteer in a school or classroom.

HABITS FOR UNITY   **Become Involved** *in July*   Patriot Red

JULY 2

TODAY... I honor my habit to BECOME INVOLVED

What are some excuses for not getting involved? Maybe it's because it is raining, or it's too hot, or it's too cold, or you don't have enough time right now, or you are low on money, or no one invited you, or you'll miss your favorite TV program, or your clothes are not expensive, or because you really WILL do it LATER.

> *Turn off the TV, turn off the CD player, and do something for your family, for your community, for yourself.*
> — **Micky Dolenz, Singer-Actor, The Monkees**

Volunteer in or just visit a nursing home.

JULY 3
TODAY... I honor my habit to BECOME INVOLVED

Don't quote me on this, but I read somewhere that less than 20% of Americans are involved as volunteers. Yet, there is so much suffering - it's easy to see that more of us are needed to help out in some way. What would happen if the other 80% gave time to help others? Which category are you? Which category do you want to be in?

> *One of America's biggest problems is not simply bad people who do wrong, but good people who do nothing.*
> **— Ted Lindeman, WWII Pilot**

> *If you're not part of the solution, you're part of the problem.*
>
> **— Eldridge Cleaver**

Take care of children for a young neighbor mother who needs a few hours to herself.

HABITS FOR UNITY   **Become Involved** *in July*   Patriot Red

JULY 4
TODAY... I honor my habit to BECOME INVOLVED

Today is the Fourth of July. Today, we all remember to stay home from work and find the nearest fireworks display. Let's remember too, that our Declaration of Independence was signed on July 4, 1776. What if our forefathers had not become involved in the pursuit of freedom and liberty? They risked their lives to sign a document that founded the United States of America.

> *And so, my fellow Americans, ask not what your country can do for you – ask what you can do for your country. My fellow citizens of the world, ask not what America will do for you, but what we together will do for the freedom of man.*
> **— John F. Kennedy, 35th President of the US**

Is there a community event or a festival that could use your help?

JULY 5

TODAY... I honor my habit to BECOME INVOLVED

Sometimes becoming involved takes courage. How many crimes are prevented by people who have the courage to step in and help? How many crimes succeed because people don't do anything? It took courage to lead our nation to freedom from tyranny in 1776. Sometimes it takes courage to help a friend by telling them your honest opinion of their actions or deeds.

> *With a firm reliance on the protection of Divine Providence, we mutually pledge to each other our lives, our fortunes, and our sacred honor.*
> **— Thomas Jefferson, Third President of the US**

Participate in Block Watch or a neighborhood safety program.

HABITS FOR UNITY   **Become Involved** *in July*   Patriot Red

JULY 6

TODAY... I honor my habit to BECOME INVOLVED

Just "speaking up" is all it takes to become involved enough to make a difference. Is there something going on in your life that needs you to speak up?

> *In Germany, the Nazis came for the Communists and I didn't speak up because I was not a Communist. Then they came for the Jews and I didn't speak up because I was not a Jew. Then they came for the trade unionists and I did not speak up because I was not a trade unionist. Then they came for the Catholics and I was a Protestant so I did not speak up. Then they came for me.*
>
> *By that time, there was no one left to speak up for anyone.*
> **— Martin Niemoller, German Theologian**

Become involved with a community service organization like Kiwanis or Rotary.

JULY 7

TODAY... I honor my habit to BECOME INVOLVED

Why wait for tragedies to happen before we get involved? Why let "getting involved" slip away when the urgency of a disaster is dissipated? If you became involved because of an immediate tragedy or disaster, turn the motivation into a long-term habit to STAY involved.

> *Motivation is what gets you started. Habit is what keeps you going.*
> — **Jim Ryun, American Distance Runner**

> *To say, yes, you have to sweat and roll up your sleeves and plunge both hands into life up to the elbows. It is easier to say no.*
> — **Jean Anouilh**

Volunteer with the Red Cross.

HABITS FOR UNITY   **Become Involved** *in July*   Patriot Red

JULY 8

TODAY... I honor my habit to BECOME INVOLVED

The gift of our environment is a treasure we too often take for granted. Our founding fathers wrote a "Bill of Rights" but not a "Bill of Responsibilities." Our rights include responsibilities that we can't ignore. Consider the hungry birds in winter or endangered animal species. They need human support to remain among us for our children to enjoy someday.

> *Say 'Yes' to the seedlings and a giant forest cleaves the sky.*
> *Say 'Yes' to the universe and the planets become your neighbors. Say 'Yes' to dreams of love and freedom.*
> *It is the password to utopia.*
> — **Brooks Atkinson**

Find an environmental cause and do something about it—or simply plant a tree.

JULY 9

TODAY... I honor my habit to BECOME INVOLVED

One of the neatest truths about volunteering is that it is both noble and selfish. In recent years, Habitat for Humanity has become very popular for volunteers. They know that there is joy in working together with others. Rubbing the shoulder of a fellow volunteer as you work side by side, can be one of the sweetest moments of the day. Be selfish. Become a volunteer.

> *The great difference between voyages rests not with the ships, but with the people you meet on them.*
> **— Amelia Barr, All the Days of My Life**

Volunteer with Habitat for Humanity.
Experience the joy of working for good.

HABITS FOR UNITY | **Become Involved** *in July* | **Patriot Red**

JULY 10

TODAY... I honor my habit to BECOME INVOLVED

Imagine what it would be like if you couldn't enjoy the rich adventure of reading. In your community, there are people who cannot read. If reading is a special enjoyment of yours, then perhaps helping an adult or a child with reading skills would bring you pleasure too. Share your love of reading. Become involved.

> *Through books...ideas find their way to the human brains, and ideals to human hearts and souls.*
> **— Dorothy Canfield Fisher**

> *Five years from now, you will be pretty much the same as you are today except for two things: the books you read and the people you get close to.*
> **— Charles Jones**

Volunteer in an adult literacy program or read to a child.

JULY 11
TODAY... I honor my habit to BECOME INVOLVED

Ask a teacher what you can do to make a difference while still lying on your bed? Teachers will tell you that many papers are graded, many lesson plans written and many tests are scored during those "ought to be my own time" moments, even in bed. What time "ought to be your own?" When is it better to give time away?

> *I think even lying on my bed*
> *I can still do something.*
> — **Dorothea Dix**

While lying in bed, think about how you would like to make a difference?

HABITS FOR UNITY   **Become Involved** *in* **July**   Patriot Red

JULY 12
TODAY... I honor my habit to BECOME INVOLVED

The arts help touch the heart and interpret those deep shared "knowings" that bring us together in spirit and love. Music and art can change our perspective and blend our points of view into one perspective of beauty.

> *The artistic innovator is perhaps our society's most valuable citizen. He or she does not so much change the world, as change how we view it. They are ambassadors of peace and advocates of understanding. They melt our differences into the common ground of the dance floor, the theater, the concert hall, and a million living rooms across the nation. That is why it is important that we so diligently search for them.*
> — **Ossie Davis, American Actor**

Volunteer to help the arts, support a theater, or an art museum or an orchestra.

JULY 13

TODAY... I honor my habit to BECOME INVOLVED

We are a country of sports spectators—which is great. We aren't all qualified to play, and yet we can all enjoy the thrill of winning. When it comes to making a difference and getting involved, however, there is a place or two—down on the field—that each of us needs to fill. When we don't take our position, someone or something somewhere, loses.

> *You must get involved to make an impact. No one is impressed with the won-lost record of the referee.*
> — **John H. Holcomb, The Militant Moderate**

Volunteer to coach or help out a children's sports team.

HABITS FOR UNITY   **Become Involved** *in July*   Patriot Red

JULY 14

TODAY... I honor my habit to BECOME INVOLVED

It seems like the motto of America today is "more is better." When was the last time you bought an item of clothing that you actually needed? I know I will never really need a new dress. What would happen to hunger and poverty if we all focused on making a differ-ence more than on making a buck? They are not mutually exclusive and they can both be done well.

> *Our greatness is built upon our freedom. It is moral, not material. We have a great ardor for gain: but we have a deep passion for the rights of man.*
> — **Woodrow Wilson, 28th President of the US**

> *It's easy to make a buck. It's a lot tougher to make a difference.*
> — **Tom Brokaw, American Journalist**

Volunteer at a shelter or a soup kitchen.
Notice that "less isn't so great."

JULY 15
TODAY... I honor my habit to BECOME INVOLVED

One of the problems with a democracy is that someone gets elected even if they don't represent most of the people. Theoretically, this only happens when people don't vote or don't educate themselves about the candidates. Then they are not represented. Become involved in making sure you know who is running for political offices and that you vote.

> *He serves his party best who serves his country best.*
> — **Rutherford B. Hayes, 19th President of the US**

> *A politician thinks of the next election; a statesman thinks of the next generation.*
> — **James Freeman Clarke**

Plan to volunteer at a voting booth in your ward or precinct— and of course—plan ahead to VOTE.

HABITS FOR UNITY   **Become Involved** *in July*   **Patriot Red**

JULY 16
TODAY... I honor my habit to BECOME INVOLVED

Mental reminders and good intentions won't replace involvement that is motivated from within your heart and spirit. This is what "being connected" is all about. Think about your relationship with your worship or ethical community. Today, think deeply, from your heart and spirit. Look at others from your heart. What do you see?

> *Trust in God* and do something.*
> — **Mary Lyon**

> *Something or someone larger than yourself

> *The gift you have received, give as a gift.*
> — **Matthew 10:8, New American Bible**

Become involved with your place of gathering or worship.

JULY 17

TODAY... I honor my habit to BECOME INVOLVED

I saw a billboard the other day - I wish I knew who put it there. It held the following message displayed as though it were signed by God. It read, "That love thy neighbor thing... I meant that." — GOD

> *The condition upon which God hath given liberty to man is eternal vigilance.*
> — **John Philpot Curran**

> *Being a good neighbor is an art which makes life richer.*
> —**Eve Birch, Librarian**

Walk down the street today with love in your heart for your neighbor.

HABITS FOR UNITY   **Become Involved** *in July*   Patriot Red

JULY 18

TODAY... I honor my habit to BECOME INVOLVED

As one person, it is easy to remain uninvolved because you think you can't make a difference. Think about this: how many people did you interact with in some way or other yesterday? If you left your home at all, your answer is probably between ten and twenty or more. In a week, this number reaches to more than 100 and, in a month,... well, you get the point.

> *We ourselves feel that what we are doing is just a drop in the ocean. But the ocean would be less because of that missing drop.*
> — **Mother Teresa, Founder, Missionaries of Charity**

Add "something better" to each of your interactions today, even if just a smile.

JULY 19
TODAY...I honor my habit to BECOME INVOLVED

Sometimes there's a fine line between the activist who gets involved by speaking up for change, and the "all talk" naysayer who never makes things better—only worse—with the noise of his/her voice. Be an "activist" for what you believe in—support a positive plan for improvement.

> *The human race is divided into two classes -- those who go ahead and do something and those who sit still and inquire, 'Why wasn't it done the other way?'*
> — **Oliver Wendell Holmes, American Author**

> *The activist is not the man who calls the river dirty. The activist is the man who cleans up the river.*
> — **H. Ross Perot, American Businessman**

Attend a community meeting where an important issue is in discussion. Add your constructive opinion, volunteer for a committee, or do research on your own.

HABITS FOR UNITY  Patriot Red

JULY 20
TODAY... I honor my habit to BECOME INVOLVED

Activism is not often popular. When great changes have been needed in our democratic society, the courageous people—like Rosa Parks, who sat down at the front of a bus for what was right—suffered greatly.

> *I want every American free to stand up for his rights, even if sometimes he has to sit down for them.*
> — **John F. Kennedy, 35th President of the US**

> *To sin by silence when they should protest makes cowards out of men.*
> — **Abraham Lincoln, 16th President of the US**

If you truly believe in an issue, take a stand for it—even if it's unpopular.

JULY 21

TODAY... I honor my habit to BECOME INVOLVED

In this patriotic month of July with 20 days of "Become Involved" behind us, it's time to up the game and suggest that becoming involved is a responsibility. Every person must become involved as a voter and as a steward of freedom so that democracy works for everyone - not just for people with power.

> *What you ought to do, you should do;*
> *and what you should do, you ought to do!*
>   — **Oprah Winfrey, Talk-Show Host and Actress**

> *Honey, it's so easy to talk a good game.*
> *What we need are folks who will do something.*
>   — **Maxine Waters, American Gospel Singer**

Spend one hour today (60 minutes) making a difference. This is a free country. You decide how!

HABITS FOR UNITY   **Become Involved** *in July*   **Patriot Red**

JULY 22

TODAY... I honor my habit to BECOME INVOLVED

One of the best things about spending your time as a volunteer is that the influence of your effort spreads out and is multiplied. Have you ever dropped a stone into a pond and watched the ripples?

> *All work is as seed sown; it grows and spreads,*
> *and sows itself anew.*
>   — **Thomas Carlyle**

> *That's what being young is all about. You have the courage and*
> *the daring to think that you can make a difference.*
>   — **Ruby Dee, American Actress**

Volunteer to do phone recruiting for United Way.

JULY 23
TODAY... I honor my habit to BECOME INVOLVED

The Rotarians motto is "Service Above Self." I've been a member of Rotary International for more than 30 years. In 2006-07 they sponsored my trip to Rwanda where I shared these 12 habits for peace and unity with educators across the country.

> *Service is where love is. Our work brings people face to face with love.*
> — **Mother Teresa, Founder, Missionaries of Charity**

> *It is by believing, hoping, loving, and doing that man finds joy and peace.*
> — **John Lancaster Spalding**

Take a few minutes today to learn more about Rotary Clubs and all the good they do for your community.
Consider joining.

HABITS FOR UNITY   **Become Involved** *in July*   Patriot Red

JULY 24
TODAY... I honor my habit to BECOME INVOLVED

A few days ago, I suggested you spend 60 minutes making a difference of your choice. Civic commitment is even better when it's long term. General Colin Powell (Ret.) heads a national movement called America's Promise—Alliance for Youth. They have hundreds of volunteer opportunities, from becoming a mentor to starting an after-school program for teens.

> *Those who expect to reap the blessings of freedom must undergo the fatigue of supporting it.*
> — **Thomas Paine**

> *A community is like a ship; everyone ought to be prepared to take the helm.*
> — **Henrik Ibsen, Playwright, An Enemy of the People**

Contact America's Promise—Website: www.americaspromise.org

JULY 25

TODAY... I honor my habit to BECOME INVOLVED

Serve quietly.

> *The world is divided into people who do things and people who get the credit. Try, if you can, to belong to the first class. There's far less competition.*
> — **Dwight Morrow**

> *Be a fountain, not a drain.*
> — **Rex Hudler**

Make an anonymous contribution
to your favorite charity.

HABITS FOR UNITY | Become Involved in July | Patriot Red

JULY 26

TODAY... I honor my habit to BECOME INVOLVED

Youth are 20% of the present and 100% of our future. We are 100% of our own future. Our future starts in the next 30 seconds.

> *Our sons and daughters must be trained in national service, taught to give as well as to receive.*
> — **Emmeline Pankhurst**

> *We should all be concerned about the future because we will have to spend the rest of our lives there.*
> — **Charles F. Kettering, Seed for Thought**

Call and volunteer at a local food bank in your area.

JULY 27
TODAY... I honor my habit to BECOME INVOLVED

There are many kids today who have never heard of Helen Keller (1880–1968). Blind and deaf from birth, she learned to speak, read, and write. She traveled and lectured to millions of people around the world. She became an inspiration for what one person who is determined can do.

> *Do not let what you cannot do interfere with what you can do.*
> — **John Wooden, Former Basketball Coach, U.C.L.A.**

> *You give but little when you give one of your possessions.*
> *It is when you give of yourself that you truly give.*
> — **Kahlil Gibran, The Prophet**

Consider volunteering at a school for the handicapped or at a blind center.

HABITS FOR UNITY   **Become Involved** *in July*   **Patriot Red**

JULY 28
TODAY... I honor my habit to BECOME INVOLVED

Dr. Wayne Dyer was a famous national lecturer and author. He would tell his audiences that he has a suit in his closet with the pockets cut off so he remembers that he won't "take it with him." Not one of us owns anything—except our own heart and soul.

> *We are here to add what we can to,*
> *not to get what we can from, life.*
> — **Sir William Osler**

> *As for me, prizes mean nothing. My prize is my work.*
> — **Katharine Hepburn, American Actress**

> *We work to become, not to acquire.*
> — **Albert Hubbard**

Take the next check that comes in the mail and give it away.

JULY 29

TODAY... I honor my habit to BECOME INVOLVED

I heard a remarkable story about the funeral of a man who died in Columbia, SC. He wrote a book, The Secret of a Happy Life, but had never sold any copies. His last wish was for the book to be distributed at his funeral. He was a happy man who had been loved by many throughout his life.

The funeral was attended by hundreds of grateful mourners. The greatly anticipated book was passed out at the end of the ceremony. Most likely it became the first book in history ever to have been read in its entirety by every recipient. Inside the book was one word: "SERVICE."

> *The roots of happiness grow best in the soil of service.*
> **— Ruth B. Love**

While you are volunteering, look into the faces around you and know you are appreciated.

HABITS FOR UNITY   **Become Involved** in *July*   Patriot Red

JULY 30

TODAY... I honor my habit to BECOME INVOLVED

> *How will you measure success in your life? Take time to step back from the crowd — the ones that value making a killing on the stock market or beating out a partner in a deal. There IS great value in capitalism and in democracy and in the American Dream — as long as it is not hiding as American Greed. Accumulate the riches of service, love, family and friends. I must admit that I personally measure success in terms of the contributions an individual makes to his or her fellow human beings.*
> **— Margaret Mead, American Anthropologist**

Does a family member or friend need some help?
Can you find time to get involved?

JULY 31
TODAY... I honor my habit to BECOME INVOLVED

It's the last day of July. It's monthly habit-building assessment day. If you are already a volunteer or a regular supporter of a charity or a cause that is important to you - then praise be to you. Thank goodness for you. You are playing your part in the unifying picture of community. If you are not committed, please evaluate the idea of volunteering once again. Somehow, somewhere, you are needed and you can make a caring difference.

Happiness consists in activity – it is a running stream, not a stagnant pool.
   — John Mason Good

If anyone thinks he has no responsibilities, it is because he has not sought them out.
   — Mary Lyon

Either thank yourself for the service you do—or think again about seeking out your own special way to become involved.

HABITS FOR UNITY   **Become Involved** *in* **July**   **Patriot Red**

The local grocery, Food Lion, in Morgan County, WV, posted July's community poster to "Become Involved," and also posted a "Become Involved," make-it-your-self poster from a local school student.

August is Month 8

KNOW WHO YOU ARE

IN AUGUST... and all year long...

Color Cue — Thoughtful Blue

Health Focus — Health Education and Immunizations

Daily Affirmation – TODAY I reflect on my habit to
KNOW WHO I AM

"Together we heal the country we all share"

— Elaine Parke

In AUGUST REMEMBER TO...
KNOW WHO I AM

This above all, to thine own self be true

And it must follow as the night the day

Thou canst not then be false to any man.
   — **William Shakespeare, British Playwright, Hamlet**

August is the summation of 12 Habits of Unity the month to evaluate who you are and how well you "walk your talk." When each of us is becoming our better selves, then we are also becoming more unified in America. We are increasing our focus on what we have in common – while honoring the ways in which we are different.

August is a slower paced month of vacations—a time to relax and also to reflect. Your habit-building color for this month is "Thoughtful Blue." Encourage yourself in August to reflect on your values and where "you" are taking your own future.

What kind of memories are you making out of your own moments? Who are you? How are you different from a year ago? And how do you want to be different a year from now? Reflect on your priorities, your direction and your values. Do you allocate your time to support what is important to you?

With appreciation to the Ty Ling Fortune Cookie Company, I have ended each August day's inspiration with a fortune cookie philosophy message. They can inspire a fleeting moment of introspection?

Goal for the Month:
Be able to write down your own values about family, children, personal behavior, work performance and your role in your community.

"Together we heal the country we all share."
--Elaine Parke

In August, Remember to..... Know Who You Are!

Truths for Living

The more generous we are,
the more joyous we become.

The more cooperative we are,
the more valuable we become.

The more enthusiastic we are,
the more productive we become.

The more serving we are,
the more prosperous we become.

The more outgoing we are,
the more helpful we become.

The more curious we are,
the more creative we become.

The more patient we are,
the more understanding we become.

The more persistent we are,
the more successful we become.

— William Arthur Ward,
American Motivational Writer

AUGUST 1

I reflect on my habit to KNOW WHO I AM

"Treat others as you want others to treat you." This is the Golden Rule of mutual respect. This great principle for happiness is found in every book of every world religion. In a month dedicated to building the habit of self-reflection, this is a time to reflect on The Golden Rule and how each moment of your life supports the Rule.

> *Practicing the Golden Rule is not a sacrifice, it's an investment.*
> — **Bylle Avery, Health Care Activist**

> *When your values are clear to you, making decisions becomes easier.*
> —**Walt Disney, Creator of Mickey Mouse**

Fortune Cookie: You are in for an enlightening experience.

HABITS FOR UNITY   **KNOW WHO YOU ARE** *in August*   **Blue**

AUGUST 2

I reflect on my habit to KNOW WHO I AM

Consider the idea that "prayer" is talking to God and "meditation" is listening. Inside of each of us is a conscience known to many as God. When we listen to it, this inner voice guides us toward happiness. Practice both prayer and meditation this month. Try reading a meditation book or simply begin each day with the practice of sitting a few moments. Quiet your thoughts so that your inner-voice can be heard.

> *Two things hold me in awe: the starry heaven above me; and the moral law within me.*
> — **Immanuel Kant, Philosopher**

> *Look well into thyself: there is a source of strength that will always spring up if thou wilt always look there.*
> — **Marcus Aurelius**

Fortune Cookie: The courage to be great lies deep within each of us.

AUGUST 3
I reflect on my habit to KNOW WHO I AM

With more than 1,100 self-help books currently in print, it is obvious that the search for happiness is a flourishing business. Why do we search for answers from someone else or in a book? Reflect on the answers you know would make you happier. How can you bring them alive in your own life?

> *Life is rather like a can of sardines—we're all looking for the key.*
> — **Alan Bennet**

> *Most people will search high and wide for the key to success. If they only knew the key to their dreams lies within.*
> — **George Washington Carver, American Scientist**

Fortune Cookie: Your eyes will be opened to a world full of love, beauty and adventure.

HABITS FOR UNITY   KNOW WHO YOU ARE™ in *August*   **Blue**

AUGUST 4
I reflect on my habit to KNOW WHO I AM

There is no purpose in life more valuable than parenting. Today, reflect on who you are in the eyes of your children (of any age). What are you teaching them?

> *The best thing you can give your children are good values, good memories and good food. Good character, like good food, is usually homemade.*
> — **Anonymous**

> *I tell Michael, 'Let them know what your priorities are: God, family, doing right, respect.' These are the things that are important in life.*
> — **Deloris Jordan, Mother of Basketball's Michael Jordan**

> *I have a dream that my four little children will one day live in a nation where they will not be judged by the color of their skin, but by the content of their character.*
> — **Martin Luther King, Jr.**

Fortune Cookie: A small gift can bring joy to the whole family.

AUGUST 5

I reflect on my habit to KNOW WHO I AM

> *The best index to a person's character is (a) how he(she) treats people who can't do him (her) any good, and (b) how he(she) treats people who can't fight back.*
> — Abigail Van Buren, Advice Columnist

> *One isn't born one's self. One is born with a mass of expectations, a mass of other people's ideas—and you have to work through it all.*
> — V. S. Naipaul

> *You have to start knowing yourself so well that you begin to know other people. A piece of us is in every person we can ever meet.*
> — John D. MacDonald, American writer

Fortune Cookie: You are open and honest in your philosophy of love.

KNOW WHO YOU ARE in *August*

HABITS FOR UNITY   **Blue**

AUGUST 6

I reflect on my habit to KNOW WHO I AM

Lifting up yourself through reading is free. Did you know that less than 31% of the American public have library cards? Have you outgrown your thirst for knowledge and education as a source of personal fulfillment? What would you like to learn more about? Why?

> *Education has for its object the formation of character.*
> — Herbert Spencer, Philosopher

> *It's not about who reaches the summit the fastest; it's who learns the most about herself (himself) along the way.*
> — Brandi Sherwood, Miss U.S.A. 1997

> *There are...two educations. One should teach us how to make a living and the other how to live.*
> — James Truslow Adams

Fortune Cookie: Advancement will come with hard work.

AUGUST 7
I reflect on my habit to KNOW WHO I AM

For many of us, reflecting on our mistakes is an obsession. People with low self-esteem often worry too much about what other people think of them. The question is: Does your reflection make you feel bad or make you a better person in the future?

When you make a mistake, admit it. If you don't, you only make matters worse.
— **Ward Cleaver, Leave it to Beaver**

When you make a mistake, acknowledge it. Know that you cannot go back. Ask for a pardon. Discover what you learned. Behave like you learned it. Go on, better than before.
— **Elaine Parke, Author**

Fortune Cookie: Past experience: He who never makes mistakes never did anything that's worthy.

HABITS FOR UNITY   KNOW WHO YOU ARE™ in *August*   **Blue**

AUGUST 8
I reflect on my habit to KNOW WHO I AM

If I could back up the clock, I would reprogram myself with more wisdom. For better or worse, our memories are the fabric of future thoughts. Memories haunt or hallow our minds - they depress or uplift our souls; they bring joy or sadness to our hearts.

Make the kind of memories that you can live with the rest of your life.
— **Anonymous**

You never know when you're making a memory.
— **Lee Jones, American Singer, "Young Blood"**

Remember wherever you go, there you are.
— **Peter Weller. "The Adventures of Buckaroo Banzai"**

Fortune Cookie: You must always have old memories and young hopes.

AUGUST 9

I reflect on my habit to KNOW WHO I AM

What brand of car do you drive, what shoe do you wear, what brand symbol is on your clothes? What is prestige?

> *If you only want to have more and more, if your idol is profit and pleasure, remember that man's value is not measured by what he has, but by what he is.*
> — **Pope John Paul II, Address to Indians of Amazonia, June, 1980**

> *No race can prosper till it learns that there is as much dignity in tilling a field as in writing a poem.*
> — **Booker T. Washington, Author, Up from Slavery**

> *I've always wanted to be somebody, but I see now I should have been more specific.*
> — **Lily Tomlin, American Actress-Comedienne**

Fortune Cookie: How you look depends on where you go.

HABITS FOR UNITY   KNOW WHO YOU ARE in August   Blue

AUGUST 10

I reflect on my habit to KNOW WHO I AM

What does success mean in your life?

> *Of all the qualities necessary for success, none comes before character.*
> — **Ernesta Procope**

> *Success is always temporary. When all is said is done, the only thing you'll have left is your character.*
> — **Vince Gill, American Country Singer**

> *You can have money and material things, but people - that's what really matters in life.*
> — **John Travolta**

Fortune Cookie: He who knows he has enough is rich.

AUGUST 11
I reflect on my habit to KNOW WHO I AM

Wouldn't it be neat to actually find an article in a woman's magazine about this kind of beauty?

> *Character contributes to beauty. It fortifies a woman as her youth fades. A mode of conduct, a standard of courage, discipline, fortitude, and integrity can do a great deal to make a woman beautiful.*
> — **Jacqueline Bissett, British Actress**

> *After a certain number of years, our faces become our biographies.*
> — **Cynthia Ozick, The Paris Review**

Fortune Cookie: Everything has beauty but not everyone sees it.

HABITS FOR UNITY   KNOW WHO YOU ARE in *August*   Blue

AUGUST 12
I reflect on my habit to KNOW WHO I AM

It doesn't take much self-examination to know that we are not qualified to judge others. Then why do we spend so much time doing it? Take time this month to develop your ability to constructively criticize yourself.

> *It is much more difficult to judge oneself than to judge others.*
> — **Antoine de Saint-Exupéry, Author, The Little Prince**

> *Two things are bad for the heart - running upstairs and running-down people.*
> — **Bernard M. Baruch, Israli Statesman**

Fortune Cookie: The care and sensitivity you show towards others will return to you.

AUGUST 13

I reflect on my habit to KNOW WHO I AM

Psychologists and educators agree that lack of self-confidence and self-worth lies at the heart of many problems people have. Knowing yourself increases your capacity for personal strength and your chance for happiness.

> *A man (woman) cannot be comfortable without his own approval.*
> — Mark Twain, American Author and Essayist

> *Not all of us have to possess earthshaking talent. Just common sense and love will do.*
> — Myrtle Auvil, West Virginia author

Fortune Cookie: A friend is a present you give to yourself.

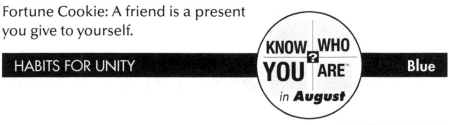

HABITS FOR UNITY   KNOW WHO YOU ARE in August   Blue

AUGUST 14

I reflect on my habit to KNOW WHO I AM

Adversity strikes every life. The weak despair in self-deceit, thinking that they alone are dealt this hand of woe.

> *Only when a tree has fallen can you take the measure of it. It is the same with a man (person).*
> — Anne Morrow Lindbergh, American Author

Habit-Building

> *Out of our beliefs are born deeds,*
> *Out of our deeds we form habits;*
> *Out of our habits grow our character;*
> *And on our character, we build our destiny.*
> — Henry Hancock

Fortune Cookie: Your doubts should disappear early this month.

AUGUST 15
I reflect on my habit to KNOW WHO I AM

There is a "cumulative" quality to life that's hard to conceptualize when you are young. Many regrets would probably be erased if we thought first, about the memories being made by our words and actions.

I am the master of my fate; I am the captain of my soul.
— **William Ernest Henley**

Our deeds travel with us from afar. And what we have been makes us what we are.
— **George Eliot, British Author**

Every man is the son of his own words.
— **Miguel De Cervantes, Spanish Author**

Fortune Cookie: You are perceptive and considerate when dealing with others.

HABITS FOR UNITY   KNOW WHO YOU **?** ARE™ *in August*   **Blue**

AUGUST 16
I reflect on my habit to KNOW WHO I AM

Like our individual lives, the nature of society is also cumulative. Our social "norms" are created by the collective behaviors of the majority. That's why, when many people are practicing the 12 values in "*The Habits of Unity*," the social climate of America will improve. Choosing to step out and volunteer your time, or to advocate for change is great - and needed. However, your contribution to a better world is also being made each day, with the words and actions of your own life.

One way to make the world better is by improving yourself.
— **Willie Williams, Chief of Police, Los Angeles, CA**

World economics without world ethic is very dangerous.
— **Anonymous**

Fortune Cookie: The happiest circumstances are close to home.

AUGUST 17

I reflect on my habit to KNOW WHO I AM

We sometimes search for new answers to happiness while the real answers sit, unpracticed, in our own minds and hearts.

> *We are what we repeatedly do.*
> *Excellence then, is not an art but a habit.*
> **— Aristotle**
> *We can be thankful for what we have or complain about what we do not have. One or the other becomes a habit pattern of our own life.*
> **— Elisabeth Elliott**

> *Habits are first cobwebs, then cables.*
> **— Spanish Proverb**

Fortune Cookie: The greater part of inspiration is perspiration.

HABITS FOR UNITY   KNOW WHO YOU ARE™ *in August*   **Blue**

AUGUST 18

I reflect on my habit to KNOW WHO I AM

Who's in charge of your life - a self-determined inspired You - or the random happenings of life?

> *We are free up to the point of choice. Then the choice controls the chooser.*
> **— Mary Crowley**

> *The vital, successful people I have met all had one common characteristic. They had a plan.*
> **— Marilyn Van Derbur, Miss America 1958**

Fortune Cookie: Don't wait for others to open the right door for you.

AUGUST 19
I reflect on my habit to KNOW WHO I AM

For centuries, the issue of temptation has been at the heart of good and evil choices. Temptation is powerful. The progress of inspired morality throughout society has been slow. Perhaps the search for new answers to happiness goes on because we don't exercise the courage and self-discipline needed to practice time-honored answers like the Golden Rule.

> *Temptation is sure to ring your doorbell, but don't ask it to stay for dinner.*
> **— Anonymous**

> *A talent is formed in stillness, a character in the world's torrent.*
> **— Johann Wolfgang Von Goethe, German Author**

Fortune Cookie: If you are still tempted, have another fortune cookie.

HABITS FOR UNITY   Blue

AUGUST 20
I reflect on my habit to KNOW WHO I AM

> *Instead of harping on a man's (person's) faults, tell him of his virtues. Try to pull him out of his rut of bad habits. Hold him up to his better self, his real self that can dare and do and win out!*
> **— Eleanor H. Porter, American Author, Pollyanna**

> *Some people change jobs, spouses, and friends—but never think of changing themselves.*
> **— Paula Giddings**

Fortune Cookie: Your skills will accomplish what the force of many cannot.

AUGUST 21

I reflect on my habit to KNOW WHO I AM

Look around you. Unless you are in a woods surrounded by pure nature, you are surrounded by items that were once ideas and beliefs that began someone's mind and heart. Every great invention was at first a frail idea. What do you believe in? What frail idea can you contribute?

> *We are what we believe we are.*
> — **Benjamin N. Cardozo, Former Supreme Court Justice**

> *In search of my mother's garden, I found my own.*
> — **Alice Walker, American Author**

Fortune Cookie: Being the first to try something new could make you great.

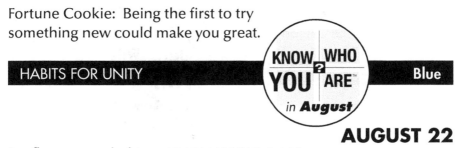

HABITS FOR UNITY   **Blue**

AUGUST 22

I reflect on my habit to KNOW WHO I AM

Keep a balance in life between pride and humility. Knowing yourself helps keep that balance steady, despite what happens day to day.

> *Most of us ask for advice when we know the answer, but want a different one.*
> — **Ivern Ball, National Enquirer**

> *Life is a long lesson in humility.*
> — **Sir James M. Barrie, British Author**

> *Success can make you go one of two ways. It can make you a prima donna, or it can smooth the edges, take away the insecurities, let the nice things come out.*
> — **Barbara Walters, American Journalist**

Fortune Cookie: Do not let great ambitions overshadow small successes.

AUGUST 23
I reflect on my habit to KNOW WHO I AM

Reverence and awe are a great source of joy. A sense of blissful wonder about the greatness of God is what spiritual commitment is about. Reverence is our best source of humility. How can ego reign in the presence of God?

> *If a man loses reverence for any part of life, he will soon lose reverence for all life.*
> — **Albert Schweitzer, Physician**

> *Our life is a faint tracing on the surface of mystery.*
> — **Annie Dillard, Author**

> *The things that we love tell us what we are.*
> — **St. Thomas Aquinas**

Fortune Cookie: Today is a perfect day to give that special person a gift.

HABITS FOR UNITY   Blue

AUGUST 24
I reflect on my habit to KNOW WHO I AM

My own personal life's nemesis has been the need to please others. For me, I should use today's reminder for at least two or three days. This will give me a little more time to remember that my polar star is my character and my conscience—not the good opinion of others.

> *Virtue is like the polar star, which keeps its place, and all stars turn towards it.*
> — **Confucius, Chinese Philosopher**

> *Virtue is the truest nobility.*
> — **Miguel De Cervantes, Spanish Author**

Fortune Cookie: Be assertive when decisive action is needed.

AUGUST 25

I reflect on my habit to KNOW WHO I AM

With the anonymity of massive social media, "Truth" has taken a real beating in recent years. Truth and virtue go hand in hand. Of all life's vicissitudes truth remains unchanged, or should, while the rest of life swirls around us. If you learn and know your own inspired truth—the rest becomes much easier. When you have learned to practice your truths, life becomes bliss.

> *Truth is great, and its effectiveness endures.*
> — **Ptahhotep, Ancient Egyptian Vizier**

> *There is no greatness where there is no simplicity, goodness and truth.*
> — **Leo Tolstoy**

Fortune Cookie:
Treasure what you have.

| HABITS FOR UNITY | KNOW WHO YOU ARE™ in *August* | Blue |

AUGUST 26

I reflect on my habit to KNOW WHO I AM

> *Character is what you know you are; not what others think you are.*
> — **Marva Collins And Civia Tamarkin, American Educators**

> *Son, when a man knows something deep down in his heart... when he really knows...he doesn't have to argue about it, doesn't have to prove it. Just knowin', that's enough.*
> — **Ben Cartwright, "Bonanza"**

> *I thought you said you've slept on rocks in the snow. I have. That's why I sleep on soft beds whenever I can.*
> — **Susan Ee, Fantasy Author, End of Days**

Fortune Cookie: Good luck is the result of good planning.

AUGUST 27
I reflect on my habit to KNOW WHO I AM

Courage is the master of temptation. Courage is the only master that you can count on when you know what is right, and temptation stands there beckoning.

Joy and courage make a handsome face.
— **French Proverb**

Life shrinks or expands in proportion to one's courage.
— **Anais Nin**

Never give in! Never give in! Never, never, never, never -- in nothing great or small, large or petty -- never give in except to conditions of honor and good sense.
— **Winston Churchill, Former British Prime Minister**

The secret of happiness is freedom, and the secret of freedom is courage.
— **Louis Brandeis, Former Supreme Court Justice**

Fortune Cookie: An exciting opportunity lies ahead if you are not timid.

HABITS FOR UNITY   Blue

AUGUST 28
I reflect on my habit to KNOW WHO I AM

A clear conscience, and making memories you can live with later, are both outcomes of a well-lived life.

A clear conscience weighs more in the scale of God and time than an empire.
— **Nikos Kazantzakis**

There is only one way to achieve happiness on this terrestrial ball, and that is to have either a clear conscience or none at all.
— **Ogden Nash, American Poet and Humorist**

Fortune Cookie: A small house, well kept, will hold as much happiness as a big one.

AUGUST 29

I reflect on my habit to KNOW WHO I AM

In the torrent of contemporary living, the concepts of compromise, temptation and virtue can easily become fuzzy. Self-reflection, prayer and constant vigilance are the keys to happiness and self-worth. You are all that you have.

> *Don't compromise yourself. You're all you've got.*
> — Janis Joplin, Singer/Songwriter

> *What you have become is the price you have paid for what you used to want.*
> — Mignon Mclaughlin

> *One's eyes are what one is, one's mouth what one becomes.*
> — John Galsworthy, British Author

Fortune Cookie: You use your creative talents to transform a business environment.

HABITS FOR UNITY   KNOW WHO YOU ARE *in August*   Blue

AUGUST 30

I reflect on my habit to KNOW WHO I AM

> *What lies before us and what lies behind us are small matters compared to what lies within us. And when we bring what is within out into the world, miracles happen.*
> — Henry David Thoreau

> *We don't know who we are until we see what we can do.*
> — Martha Grimes

> *We must all find our true purpose; like Michelangelo or Mozart or Leonardo da Vinci, each of us must develop a mission in life.*
> — Michael Jackson, American Singer

Fortune Cookie: You have a heart of gold.

AUGUST 31
I reflect on my habit to KNOW WHO I AM

Together we have written the month of August and strengthened
our habit of self-reflection and self-understanding. This month
deepens our awareness of the fabric that stabilizes and holds
together our own lives and the meaning we give to our presence
here on earth. What is the gospel according to you?

> *You write a sermon, a chapter each day By the deeds that you do
> and the words that you say; Men read what you write, if it's false
> or it's true. Say, what is the gospel according to you?*
> — **Paul Gilbert, Psychologist**

> *I may be dirty, but I have clean thoughts.*
> — **"Pig Pen," Peanuts Comic Strip**

Fortune Cookie: You are altruistic and will be
involved in many humanitarian projects.

HABITS FOR UNITY   Blue

This sign just showed up in August, in a field near Somerset, PA, when the habit for the month is, "Know Who You Are." We can't be sure it's placement was inspired by August's habit but most likely, it was.

September is Month 9

DO YOUR BEST

IN **SEPTEMBER**... and all year long...

Color Cue — AWARD Gold

Health Focus — Good Nutrition

Affirmation – TODAY, I practice my habit to DO MY BEST

"Together we heal the country we all share"

— Elaine Parke

In SEPTEMBER REMEMBER TO...
DO YOUR BEST

Kids are going back to school and vacation traffic is winding down. It's time to anchor our resolve to do well, start fresh, and begin again. This month's celebration color is "Award" GOLD." Whenever I see the color GOLD, I remember that my life and what I do with it each day is important. Whenever I see GOLD, I also remember the GOLDEN RULE.

Optimistic and positive gold, adds richness and warmth to everything—it illuminates and enhances everything. It is associated with higher ideals, wisdom, understanding and enlightenment. It inspires knowledge, spirituality and a deep understanding of the self and the "soul."

We've heard it said that "Rome wasn't built in a day." Starting something difficult or new is a great time to remember that. Writing this book, for instance, has been a glorious adventure in joy and in perseverance! It takes lots of patience and lots of practice to just "hang in there." Minutes become monuments one at a time.

Appreciation is the best reward for a job well done. There is a definite "force" in supportive words that transfer energy to the mind. Use the inspirational short stories offered every day in September to inspire you to "Do Your Own Best." In September, we celebrate our contemporaries and people down through the centuries who have contributed the best of themselves to us and to the world we share.

Goal for the month:
Pick a task, even a small one, and give it all you've got!

it couldn't be done

Somebody said that it couldn't be done,
But he with a chuckle replied
That 'maybe it couldn't,' but he would be one
Who wouldn't say so till he tried.

So, he buckled right in with the trace of a grin
On his face. If he worried, he hid it.
He started to sing as he tackled the thing
That couldn't be done, and he did it.

— Edgar A. Guest, "It Couldn't Be Done"

First time honor roll students, who "Did Their Best," at Aliquippa Middle School. After nearly two years in the prepared 12 Caring Habits environment, the school went on to win the Pennsylvania Violence-FREE Youth Award from then Governor, Tom Ridge.

SEPTEMBER 1

TODAY, I practice my habit to DO MY BEST

Andrew M. Yang (b. 1975) is an American entrepreneur, politician, and philanthropist, who ran for President in 2020. Yang believes two important components of unity are equal opportunities and the empowerment of women.

> *My parents were Taiwanese immigrants. I never thought I'd run for President. It was not on the list of careers presented to me as a skinny Asian kid growing up in New York.*
>
> **– Andrew M. Yang**

> *Tell young girls they can be anything, including entrepreneurs and self-made billionaires. We need more women solving different problems, starting companies and creating jobs to drive our economy and society forward.*
>
> **– Andrew M. Yang**

Make a habit out of empowering yourself and others!

HABITS FOR UNITY   Gold

SEPTEMBER 2

TODAY, I practice my habit to DO MY BEST

Kamala Harris (b. 1964) is the first female vice president in U.S. history. She is also the first African- American and first Asian-American vice president. She believes breaking barriers is an important component of unity.

> *My mother would look at me and say, "Kamala, you may be the first to do many things, but make sure you are not the last." That's why breaking those barriers is worth it.*
>
> **– Kamala Harris**

> *Dream with ambition, lead with conviction, and see yourself in a way that others might not see you. And we will applaud you every step of the way.*
>
> **– Kamala Harris**

Make a habit out of breaking barriers to reach your goals!

SEPTEMBER 3
TODAY, I practice my habit to DO MY BEST

Stephen Hawking (1942–2018) was an English theoretical physicist, and cosmologist. He was a recipient of the Presidential Medal of Freedom. He battled a motor neuron disease that gradually paralyzed him. He demonstrates that overcoming obstacles are important components of unity that help advance a culture.

We are all now connected by the Internet, like neurons in a giant brain.
  – **Stephen Hawking**

We are all different. There is no such thing as a standard or run-of-the mill human being, but we share the same human spirit.
  – **Stephen Hawking**

However difficult life may seem, there is always something you can do and succeed at.
  – **Stephen Hawking**

Make it your habit to support people with disabilities who overcome obstacles!

HABITS FOR UNITY   Gold

Do YOUR BEST *in September*

SEPTEMBER 4
TODAY, I practice my habit to DO MY BEST

Joseph Robinette Biden, Jr. is our 46th President and is genetically related to John Adams, the 2nd President of the United States. In his first inaugural address, President Biden appealed to our nation's leaders and citizens to heal and unify our nation. It will take everyone working together to overcome the decades-old issues that have caused America's divisions.

We can join forces, stop the shouting and lower the temperature. For without unity there is no peace, only bitterness and fury. No progress, only exhausting outrage. No nation, only a state of chaos. This is our historic moment of crisis and challenge, and unity is the path forward.
  – **Joseph R. Biden**

Encourage others to work for unity by uplifting their own lives.

SEPTEMBER 5

TODAY, I practice my habit to DO MY BEST

Ladda Tammy Duckworth is a retired Army National Guard lieutenant colonel who has served as a United States Senator from Illinois since 2017. She is the first woman with a disability elected to Congress and the first senator to give birth while in office.

> *We must be an inclusive nation that respects and supports all of its citizens; a nation that doesn't give up on anyone who doesn't give up on themselves.*
>
> **– Tammy Duckworth**

> *Sometimes it takes dealing with a disability–the trauma, the relearning, the months of rehabilitation therapy–to uncover our true abilities and how we can put them to work for us in ways we may never have imagined.*
>
> **– Tammy Duckworth**

Make it your habit to work through your challenges to find your abilities.

HABITS FOR UNITY   **Gold**

Do YOUR BEST *in September*

SEPTEMBER 6

TODAY, I practice my habit to DO MY BEST

The first President of the United States and the Commander-in-Chief of the colonial armies, George Washington, is known as the Father of Our Country. During the darkest days of his leadership, the winter at Valley Forge, our American spirit was held together with the sheer strength of Washington's character. Commanding the respect of both parties, he was elected our first president in 1789 and re-elected four years later.

> *Liberty, when it begins to take root, is a plant of rapid growth. I hope I shall always possess firmness enough to maintain what I consider the most enviable of all titles, the character of an honest man.*
>
> **— George Washington**

George Washington's life was about his citizen responsibilities more than about his rights. This is our example to follow.

SEPTEMBER 7
TODAY, I practice my habit to DO MY BEST

Until his father fled their home when he was five, James Todd Smith lived in a climate of domestic violence. At first, he grew into a violent teenager. Later, he became LL Cool J, meaning, "Ladies Love COOL James." Now he is a Grammy-winning actor and a caring husband and father.

> *Destructive behavior and a lack of focus will cause you to neglect yourself, your spirit, God and your family. I can't make sure my family is OK if I'm concentrating on the pain of my own past. I just have to forgive and get on with my life. Now I feel like I'm a winner. I've become the father I always wanted.*
> — **James Todd Smith, "LL Cool J" - reprint from USA Today - 6/98**

Turn the pains of your life into gifts you can bestow on others.

HABITS FOR UNITY	Gold

SEPTEMBER 8
TODAY, I practice my habit to DO MY BEST

Matthew McConaughey is best known as an A-list American actor and spokesman for Lincoln cars. Less known is his passion as a producer, author and philanthropist. He founded the " just keep livin' Foundation," to help teenage kids. McConaughey received the Creative Conscience award from unite4:humanity.

McConaughey's 2020 book, Greenlights is about catching more greenlights by simply changing course.

> *The problems we face today eventually turn into blessings in the rearview mirror of life. In time, yesterday's red light leads us to a greenlight. Persist, pivot, or concede. It's up to us, our choice every time.*
> – **Matthew McConaughey**

Make it your habit to make choices that help you overcome challenges.

SEPTEMBER 9

TODAY, I practice my habit to DO MY BEST

Martin Luther King, Jr., (1929–1968) is synonymous with the cause of freedom. During his life, cut short by an assassin's bullet, he lent the power of his eloquent oratory to spearhead the American Civil Rights Movement. In 1964 he became the youngest man ever to receive a Nobel Peace Prize. Like Gandhi, he espoused and practiced non-violence in the pursuit of freedom for his people.

> *When the evil plot, the good must plan. When the evil shout ugly words of hatred, the good must commit themselves to the glories of love.*
> — **Martin Luther King, Jr.**

Martin Luther King, Jr. stands as proof that great things can be accomplished regardless of the length of our tenure here on earth.

HABITS FOR UNITY — Do Your BEST in September — **Gold**

SEPTEMBER 10

TODAY, I practice my habit to DO MY BEST

Before the age of two, Helen Adams Keller (1880–1968), was deprived by illness of both her sight and hearing. She persevered to learn to write, read and speak and went on to graduate cum laude from Radcliffe College in 1904. In the face of overwhelming disabilities, the courage of Helen Keller shines as a beacon of courage and hope for all of us.

> *Keep your face to the sunshine and you cannot see the shadows.*
>
> *Life is either a daring adventure or it is nothing. Security is mostly superstition. It does not exist in nature. Avoiding danger is no safer than outright exposure.*
> — **Helen Keller**

Blindness is an affliction not just limited to the eyes. We all have blind spots that interfere with our happiness and with achieving our dreams.

SEPTEMBER 11
TODAY, I practice my habit to DO MY BEST

John F. Kennedy, the 35th President of the United States, was assassinated at the age of 46. During his short life, John Kennedy achieved military heroism in WWII, resolved the Cuban Missile Crisis, founded the Peace Corps, backed civil rights, boosted space exploration, established government support for mental health, and defied Soviet attempts to force the Allies out of Berlin.

> *And so, my fellow Americans, ask not what your country can do for you, ask what you can do for your country. The time to repair the roof is when the sun is shining.*
>
> — **John Fitzgerald Kennedy**

President Kennedy's "Ask not" quote is an eloquent statement of our times and our continuing need for citizens to practice the golden rule of responsibilities.

HABITS FOR UNITY	Gold

SEPTEMBER 12
TODAY, I practice my habit to DO MY BEST

Nelson Mandela (1918-2013), former South African President, prisoner, and political leader, was the primary force behind the ending of South African Apartheid. For the courage of his convictions, he spent more than 25 years in prison for his defiance campaign.

> *Our deepest fear is not that we are inadequate. Our deepest fear is that we are powerful beyond measure. It is our light, not our darkness, that most frightens us. We ask ourselves, 'Who am I to be brilliant, gorgeous, talented and fabulous?" Actually, who are you not to be?*
>
> *You are a child of God. You're playing small does not serve the world. There's nothing enlightened about shrinking so that other people won't feel insecure around you.*
>
> — **Nelson Rolihlahla Mandela**

Nelson Mandela speaks at a level of excellence that few can even imagine.

SEPTEMBER 13

TODAY, I practice my habit to DO MY BEST

Stacey Abrams is a voting rights activist, and author who also served in the Georgia House of Representatives. She graduated from Yale Law School, the Lyndon Johnson School of Public Affairs, and Spelman College. In February 2019, Among her many awards and honors, Stacey Abrams received a nomination for the 2021 Nobel Peace Prize for her nonviolent campaign to get out the vote.

> *We must use words to uplift and include. We can use our words to fight back against oppression and hate. But we must also channel our words into action.*
> **– Stacey Abrams**

Make it your habit to use your words to uplift, include, and bring positive change.

| HABITS FOR UNITY | Gold |

SEPTEMBER 14

TODAY, I practice my habit to DO MY BEST

John Lewis (1940 – 2020) was an American icon and beloved statesman for his persevering courage over long years of civil rights activism. He served in the U.S. Legislature for 33 years. Lewis was one of the "Big Six," leaders who organized the 1963 March on Washington. He spoke, marched, was beaten, and went to jail when necessary. During his life, John Lewis received many honorary degrees and awards, including the Presidential Medal of Freedom in 2011.

> *I believe race is too heavy a burden to carry into the 21st century. It's time to lay it down. We all came here on different ships, but now we're all in the same boat.*
> **– John Lewis**

Make it your habit to overcome the social divisions in your life.

SEPTEMBER 15
TODAY, I practice my habit to DO MY BEST

Bursting on the national scene as the poet laureate at Joseph Biden's 2021 Inauguration Ceremony, Amanda Gorman, caught the love and imagination of the nation with her haunting words and young presence. Born in 1998, she is an African-American poet and activist. Her work focuses on issues of oppression, feminism, race, and marginalization.

HABITS FOR UNITY   Gold

Her inaugural poem,
"The Hill We Climb" generated international acclaim.

> *Somehow, we've weathered and witnessed a nation that isn't broken, but simply unfinished. We, the successors of a country and a time where a skinny black girl descended from slaves and raised by a single mother can dream of becoming president only to find herself reciting for one. And yes, we are far from polished, far from pristine, but that doesn't mean we are striving to form a union that is perfect.*

> *We are striving to forge our union with purpose. To compose a country committed to all cultures, colors, characters, and conditions of man. And so, we lift our gazes not to what stands between us, but what stands before us. We close the divide because we know to put our future first, we must first put our differences aside. We lay down our arms so we can reach out our arms to one another.*

> *We seek harm to none and harmony for all. Let the globe, if nothing else, say this is true. That even as we grieved, we grew. That even as we hurt, we hoped. That even as we tired, we tried that we'll forever be tied together victorious. Not because we will never again know defeat, but because we will never again sow division.*

> **– Amanda Gorman,**
>   **Excerpt, *The Hill We Climb: An Inaugural Poem for the Country***

SEPTEMBER 16

TODAY, I practice my habit to DO MY BEST

Golda Meier (1898–1978) was a founder of the State of Israel and was its fourth Prime Minister. She emigrated from Russia to Wisconsin, where her passion ignited the Milwaukee Labor Zionist Party. She emigrated to Palestine in 1921 before becoming Prime Minister in 1969. At her death in 1978, it was revealed that she had suffered from leukemia for 12 years.

> *You cannot shake hands with a clenched fist.*

> *I can honestly say I was never affected by the question of success of an undertaking. If I felt it was the right thing to do, I was for it regardless of the possible outcome.*

> *Those who do not know how to weep with their whole heart do not know how to laugh either.*

> — **Golda Meier**

| HABITS FOR UNITY | **Do Your BEST** *in September* | Gold |

SEPTEMBER 17

TODAY, I practice my habit to DO MY BEST

Abraham Lincoln (1809–1865) preserved the United States of American through its darkest hour, the Civil War. Born in the backwoods of Kentucky, and largely self-educated, his life is a symbol of democracy and the ideal of equality. Not a physically handsome man, he was loved and admired for his inner qualities of humility, honesty, resolution, humor and courage.

> *Always bear in mind that your own resolution to succeed is more important than any other thing.*

> *I do the very best I know how - the very best I can; and I mean to keep on doing so until the end.*

> — **Abraham Lincoln**

What kills a skunk is the publicity it gives itself.

SEPTEMBER 18
TODAY, I practice my habit to DO MY BEST

Walt Disney (1901-1966) went bankrupt many times, but persevered. In 1928, he developed the cartoon character "Mickey Mouse." During the economic hard times of the 1930's, Disney's cartoons uplifted and brought joy to millions. He was the recipient of 48 Academy Awards. Walt Disney, with hard work and perseverance, made his own dreams come true.

> *Get a good idea and stay with it. Dog it, and work at it until it's done, and done right. All our dreams come true if we have the courage to pursue them.*
> — **Walt Disney**

Make your stuff into realized dreams of all sizes and shapes.

HABITS FOR UNITY   Gold

SEPTEMBER 19
TODAY, I practice my habit to DO MY BEST

Even now, the name Gandhi stands out as a worldwide synonym for courage and peaceful revolution. Mohandas (Mahatma) Gandhi (1869-1948), led the Indian Nationalist movement against British rule and is esteemed internationally for his doctrine of nonviolence to achieve political and social progress. When once asked for his "message" to the world he replied, "My life is my message." He asserted the unity of mankind under one God and preached Christian and Muslim ethics along with the Hinduism of his birth.

> *The only tyrant I accept in this world is the still voice within. No culture can survive if it attempts to be exclusive. A "no," uttered from deep conviction is better and greater than a "yes" merely said to please, or worse, to avoid trouble.*
> — **Gandhi**

SEPTEMBER 20

TODAY, I practice my habit to DO MY BEST

Dale Carnegie (1888-1955), became famous in his own lifetime by bringing out the best in others and teaching them how to be successful. His books of well-phrased rules and the teachings of the Carnegie Institute for Effective Speaking and Human Relations have helped millions. His life is an example of his own message—that success is the result of persistence, patience and personal initiative.

> *The person who goes farthest is generally the one who is willing to do and dare. The sure-thing boat never gets far from the shore.*
>
> *If you want to gather honey, don't kick over the beehive.*
>
> *When dealing with people, remember that you are not dealing with creatures of logic, but with creatures of emotion.*
>
> **—Dale Carnegie**

HABITS FOR UNITY   Gold

SEPTEMBER 21

TODAY, I practice my habit to DO MY BEST

The first Polish Pope in Catholic History, John Paul II, was the first non-Italian Pope in 456 years. Among the usual attributes of greatness John Paul's fluency in many languages qualified him well as an international ambassador for his Church. Despite an assassination attempt in 1981, his passionate commitment to spread the word of God has continued strong throughout his long tenure.

> *We must strive to multiply bread so that it suffices for all the tables of mankind.*
>
> *To maintain a joyful family requires much from both the parents and the children.*
>
> *Each member has to become, in a special way, the servant of all of the others. When freedom does not have an ethical purpose, it turns against humanity and society.*
>
> **— John Paul II**

SEPTEMBER 22
TODAY, I practice my habit to DO MY BEST

Agnes Gonxha Bojarhiu (1910-1997) was born in Skopje, Yugoslavia in 1910. In 1928, in Ireland, she joined the Institute of the Blessed Virgin Mary. Soon after, in the slums of Calcutta, she founded the Order of the Missionaries of Charity, which now numbers more than 1,000 nuns worldwide. In 1979, her gift of her own life to the poor of the world earned her the Nobel Peace Prize. Today, we know this great woman of the 20th century as Mother Teresa.

> *We can do no great things—only small things with great love. I am a little pencil in the writing hand of God who is sending a love letter to the world. A smile is the beginning of peace.*
> — **Mother Teresa**

Do the best you can in every task, no matter how unimportant it may seem at the time.

HABITS FOR UNITY   Gold

SEPTEMBER 23
TODAY, I practice my habit to DO MY BEST

Over the course of his lifetime, Vince Lombardi (1913–1970) became a national symbol for the determination to win. Born in New York City, he played and coached football at Fordham University. In 1959 he became Head Coach of the Green Bay Packers and forged a defeated team into the dominant professional team of the 1960s—winning five national NFL championships and the first two Super Bowls.

> *It's not whether you get knocked down, it's whether you get up. The difference between a successful person and others is not a lack of strength, not a lack of knowledge, but rather a lack of will. The harder you work the harder it is to surrender.*
> — **Vince Lombardi**

SEPTEMBER 24

TODAY, I practice my habit to DO MY BEST

Dolly Rebecca Parton is an American country singer, songwriter, actress, author, businesswoman, and humanitarian. She was born on January 19, 1946, one of 12 children of Avie Lee and tobacco farmer Robert Lee Parton, and grew up on a rundown farm in Tennessee. By age 12 she was appearing on Knoxville TV and at 13 she was appearing at the Grand Ole Opry.

> *"I can't stop long enough to grow old. I'm just gonna be the best that I can be at whatever age I am."*
>
> *"The way I see it, if you want the rainbow, you gotta put up with the rain."*
>
> *"It's a good thing I was born a girl, otherwise I'd be a drag queen."*
> – **Dolly Parton**

Enjoy the rain while you persevere with being the best you can.

HABITS FOR UNITY   **Gold**

SEPTEMBER 25

TODAY, I practice my habit to DO MY BEST

He never held public office, yet Benjamin Franklin (1706-1790) was one of the most famous statesmen of the ages. He is best known for his ingenuity in guiding the separation of the American colonies from Great Britain and for helping to frame the Declaration of Independence. His famous experiment with a kite in a thunderstorm proved the presence of electricity in lightning.

> *Diplomacy is the art of helping someone else have your idea. The way to see by Faith is to shut the eye of Reason. Who is wise? He that learns from everyone. Who is powerful? He that governs his passions. Who is rich? He who is content. Who is that? Nobody.*
> — **Benjamin Franklin**

Let someone else have your idea today.

SEPTEMBER 26
TODAY, I practice my habit to DO MY BEST

Susan Brownell Anthony (1820–1906) was the American leader of the women's suffrage movement. She organized the Daughters of Temperance and, with Elizabeth Cady Stanton, led the campaign for women's rights laws in New York. The laws guaranteed rights over their children and control of their property and wages. She supported President Lincoln, but opposed suffrage to freedmen without also giving it to women.

> *Failure is impossible*
> — **Susan B. Anthony**

Make your own lemons into lemonade.

Do ★ Your BEST *in September*

HABITS FOR UNITY   Gold

SEPTEMBER 27
TODAY, I practice my habit to DO MY BEST

Albert Schweitzer (1875–1965) was one of the greatest Christians and missionaries of his time. His life and writing such as "Philosophy of Civilization," exemplified a reverence for nature that may have been the harbinger of the era of environmentalism. Born in Alsace in Germany, he was a brilliant musician and an authority on the life of Bach. With proceeds from his concerts and lectures Schweitzer built a hospital in Gabon, Africa. Public acknowledgment of his selfless commitment to humanity won him the Nobel Peace Prize in 1952.

> *A man/woman is ethical, only when life, as such, is sacred to him/her. There is no higher religion than human service. To work for the common good is the greatest creed. Example is not the main thing in influencing others. It is the only thing.*
> — **Albert Schweitzer**

SEPTEMBER 28

TODAY, I practice my habit to DO MY BEST

Sir Winston Churchill (1874–1965), as a wartime prime minister, led Great Britain from the brink of defeat to victory over Hitler's aggression in Europe. He was appointed as prime minister in 1939. His refusal to make peace with Hitler was crucial to maintaining British resistance between 1940 and 1942. He joined Franklin D. Roosevelt and Joseph Stalin to shape allied strategies for the war. In 1953 he was knighted and also was awarded the Nobel Prize in literature.

> *The price of greatness is responsibility. An appeaser is one who feeds a crocodile, hoping it will eat him last. The greatest lesson in life is to know that even fools are right sometimes.*
> — **Sir Winston Churchill**

HABITS FOR UNITY **Do Your Best** *in September* Gold

SEPTEMBER 29

TODAY, I practice my habit to DO MY BEST

Henry Ford (1863–1947) was an American industrial pioneer and folk hero. His innovations changed forever the economic and social character of America... and the world. His goal was the employment of mass production techniques to make automobiles that were affordable for the average person. He raised pay for his workers above the norm of the day and began a profit-sharing plan that distributed up to $30 million a year among his employees. As a noted philanthropist, he established the Ford Foundation and the Henry Ford Museum.

> *Anyone who stops learning is old. A bore is a person who opens his mouth and puts his feats in it. Even a mistake may turn out to be the one thing necessary to a worthwhile achievement. My best friend is the person who brings out the best in me.*
> — **Henry Ford**

SEPTEMBER 30
TODAY, I practice my habit to DO MY BEST

Best known for his contributions to the field of physics, Albert Einstein (1879–1955) was considered by many to have had the greatest mind of all time. Born in Germany, the Nazi government confiscated his property and citizenship because he was Jewish. In 1940, he became an American citizen holding a post at the Institute for Advanced Studies from 1933 until his death. An ardent pacifist, he received the 1921 Nobel Prize in physics.

> *A hundred times a day I remind myself that my life depends on the labors of other people, and that I must exert myself in order to give, in the measure as I have received, and am still receiving. Try not to become a person of success but rather try to become a person of value.*
>
> **— Albert Einstein**

HABITS FOR UNITY   Gold

REMEMBER YOUR ABC's
for Doing Your Best in September

Avoid negative sources, people, place things and habits.

Believe in yourself.

Consider things from every angle.

Don't give up and don't give in.

Enjoy life today, yesterday is gone, tomorrow may never come.

Family and friends are hidden treasures, seek them and enjoy their riches.

Give more than you plan to.

Hang on to your dreams.

Ignore those who try to discourage you.

Just do it!

Keep trying no matter how hard it seems, it will get easier.

Love yourself first and most.

Make it happen.

Never lie, cheat or steal, always strike a fair deal.

Open your eyes and see things as they really are.

Practice makes perfect.

Quitters never win and winners never quit.

Read, study and learn about everything important in your life.

Stop procrastinating.

Take control of your own destiny.

Understand yourself in order to better understand others.

Visualize it.

Why? Because you are worth it.

Xcellerate your efforts.

You are unique in all God's creations, nothing or no one can replace you.

Zero in on your target and go for it!!

October is Month 10

BE PATIENT AND LISTEN

*IN **OCTOBER**... and all year long...*

Color Cue — Slow-Down Lavender

Health Focus — Safety in all things

Affirmation – TODAY, I pause for my habit to
BE PATIENT AND LISTEN

"Together we heal the country we all share."

– Elaine Parke

In OCTOBER, REMEMBER TO...
BE PATIENT AND LISTEN

Having known about and lived through the twelve-month cycle of the 12 Unity Habits for 30 years now, I welcome October as the month to rest my weary soul. I see peaceful joy in the breath-takingly colorful autumn nature show outside my home and office. I love the sense of calm and quiet appreciation of beauty that I feel under the influence of "Be Patient and Listen."

This month's celebration color is Slow-down LAVENDER. Whenever I see the color LAVENDER, I feel quieter, more tuned to listening, and more connected to those who pass through my day. Lavender encourages calmness and tranquility of mind and is useful for both self-reflection and invoking a relaxed, meditative state.

Think about being patient and listening as safety measures when you are driving. The accident statistics attributed to "road rage" are sobering. Driving is a time to remember something a friend of mine once said, "Help everyone that you can, and if you cannot help them, at least don't hurt them." Drive carefully this month, with caring and respect for others on the road with you.

Enjoy your leisurely stroll through our daily inspirations for October and pause to reflect often. Remember there is a sparkling spectrum of color in every moment, in every person, and in every autumn leaf. Let the leaves remind you to enjoy the colors of each moment and to appreciate the treasure of "moment jewels" that you will find when you are patient with yourself and listen to your heart. I've often said that life is like a bag of M&M's. Life is moments and memories. October is a month to ask yourself, "What's the worst that can happen if I don't do _____? or "Am I the only person who _____? or How bad can it be?

Goal for the Month:
Find the patience to make cherished memories out of more moments this month.

Slow Dance

Have you ever watched kids on a merry-go-round?
Or listened to the rain slapping on the ground?

Ever followed a butterfly's flight,
or gazed at the sun into the fading night?

> *You better slow down. Don't dance so fast.*
> *Time is short. The music won't last.*

Do you run through each day -- On the fly?
When you ask "How are you?" Do you hear the reply?

When the day is done, Do you lie in your bed
With the next hundred chores, Running through your head?

> *You'd better slow down. Don't dance so fast.*
> *Time is short. The music won't last.*

Ever told your child, We'll do it tomorrow?
And in your haste, Not see his sorrow?

Ever lost touch, Let a good friendship die
'Cause you never had time To call and say "Hi?"

> *You'd better slow down. Don't dance so fast.*
> *Time is short. The music won't last.*

When you run so fast to get somewhere
You miss half the fun of getting there.

When you worry and hurry through your day,
It is like an unopened gift.... Thrown away.

> *Life is not a race. Do take it slower*
> *Hear the music Before the song is over.*

— **David L. Weatherford, Child Psychologist**

OCTOBER 1

TODAY, I pause for my habit to BE PATIENT AND LISTEN

The quality of patience reflects love of self and love of others. Without patience, we miss so much of life while hurrying on to the next thing. Without patience, we miss the beauty of other people.

> *What is this life, if full of care, we have no time*
> *to stop and stare?*
> — W.H. Davies, Leisure Songs of Joy

> *...the unity that binds us all together, that makes this earth a*
> *family, and all men brothers and the sons of God, is love.*
> — Thomas Wolfe, American Author

Learn to enjoy silence.

HABITS FOR UNITY   Lavender

OCTOBER 2

TODAY, I pause for my habit to BE PATIENT AND LISTEN

The best teachers of patience are our children.

> *You can learn many things from children. How much patience*
> *you have, for instance?*
> — Franklin P. Jones

> *Loving a child doesn't mean giving in to all his whims;*
> *to love him is to bring out the best in him,*
> *to teach him to love what is difficult.*
> — Nadia Boulanger, French composer

> *Patience is the ability to count down before you blast off.*
> — Anonymous

Our children are 21% of our present and 100% of our future. Be loving and patient, and above all, listen to them.

OCTOBER 3
TODAY, I pause for my habit to BE PATIENT AND LISTEN

We know there are people who can chew gum and walk at the same time but is there anyone who can listen and talk at the same time? Sometimes we don't know when to stop talking.

A closed mouth gathers no feet.
   — **Anonymous**

You never saw a fish on the wall with its mouth shut.
   — **Sally Berger**

A closed mouth gathers no hooks.

| HABITS FOR UNITY | | Lavender |

OCTOBER 4
TODAY, I pause for my habit to BE PATIENT AND LISTEN

There IS a quiet voice inside of us that is worthy of being listened to. We have named this voice everything from intuition, to conscience, to God—but collectively we all know it is there. Take a few minutes to listen for the guidance that comes from within your own heart.

In the silence of prayer, encounter with God is activated.
   — **Pope John Paul II**

When you truly know yourself, you don't try to impress people anymore.
   —**Maxime Lagace, Canadian Hockey Player**

Everything we create in life comes from our inner silence. Give this resource time to bloom. Close your eyes and sit in silence for five minutes.

OCTOBER 5

TODAY, I pause for my habit to BE PATIENT AND LISTEN

I woke up this morning worrying about something I said yesterday.
I was kidding around with students in my 12 Habit group at school.
I jokingly "slipped" and used a slang word—and they all gasped
that Mrs. Parke had said such a thing. I realized how sensitive kids
are and how you create an image with them that is very fragile.
Then I realized that for me, this was a time for a prayer.

> *Any concern too small to be turned into a prayer*
> *is too small to be made into a burden.*
> — **Corrie Ten Boom, Clippings From My Notebook**

Feel the lightness of turning every
burden and worry into a prayer.

HABITS FOR UNITY   Lavender

OCTOBER 6

TODAY, I pause for my habit to BE PATIENT AND LISTEN

Have you heard of "road rage" and other terms that describe the
way we too often treat each other badly? Hopefully, the 12 Golden
Rule habits will help each of us remember to be more respectful
and considerate as we go through a normal day. Improving our
own sense of humor will also help.

> *Today's society will ignore almost any form of rudeness*
> *except getting in the express line with two extra items.*
> — **Paul Sweeney**

We are funny. Laugh at human nature and feel the peace
it brings forth in you.

OCTOBER 7
TODAY, I pause for my habit to BE PATIENT AND LISTEN

"Hi, How are you?"

"How's it going?"

"What's happening?"

Do you really mean it? Do you want an answer? Do you have time to listen to an answer? What do you do when someone really shares with you a problem or a burden they are carrying?

> *There is no greater gift than a sympathetic ear.*
> — Frank Tyger, Editorial Cartoonist

Today, ask someone how they are doing and then really listen to their answer.

HABITS FOR UNITY | Lavender

OCTOBER 8
TODAY, I pause for my habit to BE PATIENT AND LISTEN

The Golden Rule is all about mutual respect. Respect is best and truest when it comes from the heart. Sometimes, however, a structure of behavior involving manners, can help start a new relationship or tide you over when you don't know what else to do.

> *The great secret is not having bad manners or good manners or any other particular sort of manners, but having the same manners for all human souls.*
> — George Bernard Shaw, British Playwright

Manners are an expression of respect.

OCTOBER 9

TODAY, I pause for my habit to BE PATIENT AND LISTEN

Mass electronic media has changed the course of human history. It has turned us into a "sound-byte" generation who find it difficult to pay attention to anything for more than 30 seconds. It has also interfered with our sense of discrimination about use of time. Too often, "What's on TV?" is the plan for our evening. Pay attention this month to your use of time. Be patient enough to plan alternative activities with your family and friends that don't involve media or texting.

> *There was a good educational channel in the good old days –
> it was called "OFF."*
>
> **— Author Unknown**

Watch TV channel "OFF" this month.

HABITS FOR UNITY   *P* **BE** *atient* and **Listen** *in October*   **Lavender**

OCTOBER 10

TODAY, I pause for my habit to BE PATIENT AND LISTEN

There's an old adage " if you don't have time to do it right, do you have time to do it again?" Take time today to be thorough in your evaluation of alternatives. Find out more about your choices and determine a path based on complete understanding.

> *Be patient with life. Sometimes the road less traveled
> is less traveled for a reason.*
>
> **— Jerry Seinfeld**

Have you ever been saved from disaster because something didn't happen fast enough?

OCTOBER 11
TODAY, I pause for my habit to BE PATIENT AND LISTEN

Our "instant gratification" lifestyle is fertile ground for valuing short term gratification or what feels the best right now. Spend some time this month taking a longer-range look at your short-term choices. Sometimes you just want to get back at someone, or you get angry because someone seemed to let you down. Is your reaction just about "how you feel right this minute?"

Life is much more than how you feel right this minute.
> — **Elaine Parke, Author**

When this moment is hard to bear, remember that the continuity of living is made sweet by the variety of its landscapes: past, present, and future.

HABITS FOR UNITY   *BE Patient and* **Listen** *in October*   **Lavender**

OCTOBER 12
TODAY, I pause for my habit to BE PATIENT AND LISTEN

Patience is power. Many times, a little patience pays off. I remember moving to a new city with several job opportunities, one a great job and the other so-so. I wanted the better job, but didn't hear right back from the company. Each day that I waited, I was tempted to call and accept the other offer. Then, nearly two weeks later, the call came and the better job was mine.

He that can have patience can have what he will.
> — **Benjamin Franklin, American Patriot**

Patience is power; with time and patience the mulberry leaf becomes silk.
> — **Chinese Proverb**

Patience is the companion of wisdom.
> — **St. Augustine**

Practice quiet wisdom.

OCTOBER 13

TODAY, I pause for my habit to BE PATIENT AND LISTEN

There are many stories of great people down through the centuries who have won with patience. Firm patience is one of the essential qualities of non-violent change. Gandhi changed India with non-violence because he believed in a dynamic called "Satyagraha." It is a force that works silently and slowly. In reality, Gandhi believed that no other force in the world is so direct or so strong.

In any contest between power and patience, bet on patience.
— W.B. Prescott

Remember the patient power
of Gandhi.

HABITS FOR UNITY   Lavender

OCTOBER 14

TODAY, I pause for my habit to BE PATIENT AND LISTEN

Raising children teaches us patience in many ways. One of the challenges is to resist "doing it for them" because we can do it faster and better. Children who are not allowed to struggle with new challenges will not know how to be self-reliant as adults.

When you give someone a fish, you feed them for a day. When you teach someone to fish, you've fed them for a lifetime.
— Old Proverb

As a parent, how difficult this is to do. Without reaching for the shoestrings, patiently encourage a small child to tie his/her own shoe from beginning to end.

OCTOBER 15
TODAY, I pause for my habit to BE PATIENT AND LISTEN

Breaking up a "daunting" task into smaller pieces makes all the difference. Writing this book, for me, is a great example of that. As a former advertising copywriter, I have written "sound-byte" length copy all my life. I'm sure I have written many book-lengths of it, but never added it up. When I decided to write a book, the task seemed impossible. I thought I could never write 200 or 300 pages all at once. I treated each day as one sound-byte of writing, day by day—and sooner than I thought, the book was done.

> *Life is a trial, mile by mile, life is hard, yard by yard; but life is a cinch, inch by inch.*
> — **Old English Saying**

> *Life is entirely too time consuming.*
> — **Irene Peter**

The inches of life are its moments.

HABITS FOR UNITY   Lavender

OCTOBER 16
TODAY, I pause for my habit to BE PATIENT AND LISTEN

> *Imagine what a bridge or a building would look like if the build-ers never took time to plan first and just started building? When you take time, and are patient enough to plan, there's room for creativity to come to light. When you feel hurried or too rushed to be patient, ask yourself, is the rush or is the quality of the solution more important? No matter what difficulty you're facing, the practice of creative patience is a proven road to solutions.*
> — **Norman Vincent Peale, Clergyman and Author**

We have 1,440 minutes each day to patiently listen for the voice from within our hearts.

OCTOBER 17

TODAY, I pause for my habit to BE PATIENT AND LISTEN

Both take patience, but there is a difference between anticipation and anxious worry while we are waiting. If you find yourself worrying about something in the future, an operation or a deadline you have to meet for a project, try to think of the positive outcomes and define tasks you can do while waiting.

> *Steady, patient, persevering thinking will generally surmount every obstacle in the search after truth.*
> **— Emmons**

> *Be patient with everyone, but above all with yourself.*
> **— St. Francis de Sales**

Is patience with yourself the most difficult for you?

HABITS FOR UNITY   **Lavender**

OCTOBER 18

TODAY, I pause for my habit to BE PATIENT AND LISTEN

I wanted to find a quote from Thomas Edison about this subject. Most of us know the story of how he tried 1,000 ways to make a light bulb before he was successful. His effort is proof of the fact that the really valuable achievements in life do not come easily. The real secret to success is simply, have patience, stick with it and don't quit.

> *Genius begins great works; labor alone finishes them.*
> **— Joseph Joubert**

> *If I have ever made any valuable discoveries, it has been owing more to patient attention, than to any other talent.*
> **— Sir Isaac Newton, British Mathematician**

We fool ourselves when we allow failure to rein over perseverance.

OCTOBER 19

TODAY, I pause for my habit to BE PATIENT AND LISTEN

I'm a terrible "waiter." I've found that the best way to handle it is not to wait at all. This doesn't mean to move up the date of what you are waiting for, but to refuse to adopt a "waiting" frame of mind. Every moment has its own treasures. When we are "waiting" they are lost. Spend your moments in a "treasure-finding" instead of a "waiting" frame of mind.

> *All things come round to him who will but wait.*
> — **Henry Wadsworth Longfellow, American Poet**

> *Anticipating is even more fun*
> *than recollecting.*
> — **Malcolm S. Forbes, Sr., American Businessman**

When I feel impatient, whatever the holiday,
I remember the morning AFTER the
presents are unwrapped.

HABITS FOR UNITY   Lavender

OCTOBER 20

TODAY, I pause for my habit to BE PATIENT AND LISTEN

Why do we always expect people to be logical? How often have you found yourself saying, "I don't see why he/she did that, that made no sense, what did he/she do THAT for?" People are meant to be loved and cared for from the heart, not the mind. So often, there is more to the story than we can see from our perspective. Be patient and forgiving with others, especially children.

> *When you handle yourself, use your head;*
> *when you handle others, use your heart.*
> — **Donna Reed, The Donna Reed Show**

Handling others with your heart is easy to say
but more difficult to do—especially as a parent.

OCTOBER 21

TODAY, I pause for my habit to BE PATIENT AND LISTEN

To persevere is the first thing a child ought to learn, and that which he will have the most need to know as life unfolds. Perseverance is patience stretched out for as long as it's needed to achieve your dreams and your goals.

> *There is always one moment in childhood when the door opens and lets the future in.*
> — **Graham Greene, The Power and the Glory**

> *Rivers know this: there is no hurry. We shall get there some day.*
> — **A.A. Milne, Winnie-the-Pooh**

The future is entering every one of our 1,440 minutes, each day.

HABITS FOR UNITY   **Lavender**

OCTOBER 22

TODAY, I pause for my habit to BE PATIENT AND LISTEN

Think about how many stress-reduction, sleeping aid and digestion products are sold each day. Would we all need fewer of these products if we had the perseverance to know that uncomfortable moments will always pass if we wait patiently?

> *Patience can be bitter but its fruit is sweet.*
> — **Rosseau**

> *Unquiet meals make ill digestions. How poor are they that have not patience!*
> — **William Shakespeare, British Playwright**

Remember, Shakespeare never took a TUMS or read any stress reduction literature.

OCTOBER 23
TODAY, I pause for my habit to BE PATIENT AND LISTEN

Children learn by example and we are known by our examples. People who teach us how to influence others say that we deliver only 9% of our message with words. The rest we deliver with our gestures and our actions. Teaching patience by example is the best way to influence our children. In the car, do your children see you as patient and caring with other drivers on the road?

> *There is no such thing as preaching patience into people, unless you make the sermon so long, they have to practice while they listen.*
> — **Henry Ward Beecher**

I hope this "sermon" for October isn't too long.

HABITS FOR UNITY   Lavender

OCTOBER 24
TODAY, I pause for my habit to BE PATIENT AND LISTEN

> *In life, when you don't succeed the first time you try something, you don't just throw up your hands and say it can't be done. Being a good student takes hard work, patience, and sticking to it.*
> — **Ward Cleaver, Leave It To Beaver**

> *Be not afraid of growing slowly, be afraid only of standing still.*
> — **Chinese Proverb**

> *The key to everything is patience. You only get the chicken alive by hatching the egg, not by smashing it.*
> — **Arnold H. Glasow**

OCTOBER 25

TODAY, I pause for my habit to BE PATIENT AND LISTEN

It takes patience to be a friend.

*The most called-upon prerequisite of a friend
is an accessible ear.*
— **Maya Angelou, American Poet**

*You never really understand a person until you consider things
from his/her point of view.*
— **Harper Lee, Author, To Kill a Mockingbird**

You have 1,440 minutes today.
Make time to fully understand and
listen to a friend.

| HABITS FOR UNITY | | Lavender |

OCTOBER 26

TODAY, I pause for my habit to BE PATIENT AND LISTEN

Make this a quiet day where the world comes into your heart with
beauty and grace. Enjoy the simplicity of today.

Remember the forgotten shreds of simplicity in our quiet hearts.
— **Anonymous**

Adopt the pace of nature; her secret is patience.
—**Ralph Waldo Emerson**

Slow down, simplify and be kind.
— **Naomi Judd, American Country Singer**

Thank you, Naomi, the simplicity
of your quote puts it all together.

OCTOBER 27
TODAY, I pause for my habit to BE PATIENT AND LISTEN

Sometimes I find myself being impatient with others. I am upset when someone says to me, "Haven't you finished that report, or cleaned the kitchen yet, etc.?" Why are they questioning me, I think? I always know why it isn't done. I have to remember that if my own reasons are justifiable, then so are someone else's.

> *It's easy finding reasons why other folks should be patient.*
> — George Eliot, British Author

... especially at work when you
  are writing a report.

HABITS FOR UNITY   Lavender

OCTOBER 28
TODAY, I pause for my habit to BE PATIENT AND LISTEN

According to Peter Drucker, communication is 7% words and 93% everything else. We forget this when we can't wait to get our own opinion, story or point of view across in a conversation.

> *If you are quiet, you may hear a compliment.*
> — Chanelle, Age 12

> *You don't learn anything while you're talking.*
> — Albert Marks

> *The most important thing in communication*
> *is to hear what isn't being said.*
> — Peter F. Drucker

Make today a "practice listening" day.

OCTOBER 29

TODAY, I pause for my habit to BE PATIENT AND LISTEN

Patience is a key factor in avoiding many of the problems we have in life. How many road accidents wouldn't happen if we weren't in a hurry? How many arguments would be avoided if we waited and really thought about the point of view of another person?

> *When angry, count ten before you speak;*
> *if very angry, count to a hundred.*
> — **Thomas Jefferson, 3rd President of the US**

> *When you get to the end of your rope,*
> *tie a knot, hang on, and swing!*
> — **Leo Buscaglia**

Tie a knot at the end of your rope. Now start swinging and enjoying the ride.

HABITS FOR UNITY   *Patient* **BE** and **Listen** *in October*   **Lavender**

OCTOBER 30

TODAY, I pause for my habit to BE PATIENT AND LISTEN

Patience is a key to happiness. It is the difference between "feeling out of control" in your life, and feeling as though all things are happening in some order. Accept that we don't understand everything - but trusting in the butterfly can bring happiness to moments that otherwise would be rushed into nothingness.

> *Happiness is like a butterfly. The more you chase it, the more*
> *it will elude you. But, if you turn your attention to other things,*
> *it comes and softly sits on your shoulder.*
> — **Viktor Frankl, Holocaust Survivor and Philosopher**

Sit and watch a butterfly, if only in your imagination.

OCTOBER 31
TODAY, I pause for my habit to BE PATIENT AND LISTEN

When I was just 19, I read this passage from "Letters to a Young Poet." Since then, it has been an anchor of perspective for my entire life's journey.

> *"Have patience with everything unresolved in your heart and try to love the questions themselves as if they were glorious books of mystery. Don't search for the answers, which could not be given to you now, because you would not be able to live them. And the point is to live everything. Live the questions now. Perhaps then, someday far into the future, you will gradually, without even noticing it, live your way into the answer."*
> — **Rainer Maria Reilke, German Poet**

As we leave October, let Reilke's quote anchor us on our journey together.

| HABITS FOR UNITY | Lavender |

Student created Bulletin Board for October, "Be Patient and Listen," at South Hills Middle School in Pittsburgh, PA. If you could see the color, it is "Slow-down Lavender," to enhance our memory to practice be patient and listen.

November is Month 11

SHOW A POSITIVE ATTITUDE

IN **NOVEMBER**... and all year long...

Color Cue — SUNNY Yellow

Health Focus — Reduce Stress

Affirmation – TODAY, I find joy in my habit to
SHOW A POSITIVE ATTITUDE

"Together we heal the country we all share."

– Elaine Parke

In NOVEMBER, REMEMBER TO...
SHOW A POSITIVE ATTITUDE

This is my favorite month's habit, to Show a Positive Attitude. Our celebration color is SUNNY Yellow. Yellow is cheerful - the radiance of the day's new sun as it first rises into the morning sky. This is the month to work on our perspective about life and to share a positive attitude more often. Sometimes it is necessary to "Fake it 'til we make it."

When we do this, we often find that a "true" positive attitude will come about more quickly. Meanwhile, we've curtailed our negative ripples from spreading out to other family, friends, and co-workers. Enjoy the moments as they happen this month and especially the joy of Thanksgiving with friends and family. Make positive memories to savor again and again.

Research shows that optimists adjust better to stressful situations than people who have more negative outlooks. This means that working on your optimism and positivity is actually good for your health.

The color yellow is cheerful and stimulates our mental faculties, creating mental agility and perception. It is uplifting and illuminating, offering hope, happiness, and fun. It inspires original thought and inquisitiveness. It is the best color to create enthusiasm for life and can awaken greater confidence and optimism.

Over the years, from the internet and friends, I've collected many little short jokes or humorous children's comments. This month, to "Show a Positive Attitude," I am sharing one each day with you. If you have some "positive attitude one-liners," that you like, please visit our website – www.12habits4allofus.org - and share them with us.

GOAL for the Month of November:
On every excursion, wear JOY in your smile.

Attitude by Charles Swindoll

"The longer I live the more I realize the impact of attitude on life. Attitude, to me, is more important than
facts. It is more important than the past, than education, than money, than circumstances, than failures,
than successes, than what other people think or say
or do. It is more important than appearance, giftedness
or skill. It will make or break a company... a church
...a home.

The remarkable thing is we have a choice everyday
regarding the attitude we will embrace for that day. We
cannot change the inevitable. The only thing we can do
is play on the one string we have, and that is our attitude. I am convinced that life is 10% what happens to
me and 90% how I react to it. And so it is with you... we
are in charge of our Attitudes."

HUMOR TIPS for NOVEMBER:

Lighten up this month. A laugh at your own expense costs you nothing.

It's good to have money: but don't lose sight of the things money can't buy.

The best thing to hang onto in this world is one another.

I expect to pass through life but once. If therefore, there is any kindness I can show to others I will do it now.

Always have good thoughts: they may break into words at any time.

The person who gets ahead in this world, is the one who does more than is necessary.

The best thing about our future, is that it comes just one day at a time.

Happiness is not perfected until it is shared.

Joy comes not to him who seeks it for himself, but to him who seeks it for other people.

Share your love and your love will be returned.

The most beautiful and best things in the world cannot be seen, nor touched. They are felt in the heart.

We make a living by what we get, but we make a life by what we give.

Laughter is the brush that sweeps away the cobwebs of the heart.

    — **Mort Walker, Creator, "Beetle Bailey" Comic Strip**

"Together we heal the country we all share."
    — **Elaine Parke**

Samples of "Show a Positive Attitude Action Motivating Materials Used in Communities and schools These included, posters, bookmarks, monthly inspiration books, pencils, bracelets, table tents, rack cards, and homework planners.

NOVEMBER 1

TODAY, I find joy in my habit to SHOW A POSITIVE ATTITUDE

Humor is a great "sunshine maker." Nothing lightens us up more than a good laugh or even just a quiet chuckle. A fourth-grade teacher gave her students the first phrase of a list of famous sayings and asked them to provide original endings. You will find some of these, plus a few other jewels of humor at the end of each daily inspiration.

Lighten up this week. A laugh at your own expense
costs you nothing.
— **Anonymous**

If you want to be gloomy, there's gloom enough to keep you glum;
if you want to be happy, there's gleam enough to keep you glad.
— **Maltbie D. Babcock, American Clergyman**

The grass is always greener when
you remember to water it.

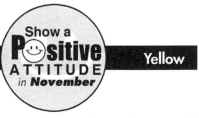

HABITS FOR UNITY   **Yellow**

NOVEMBER 2

TODAY, I find joy in my habit to SHOW A POSITIVE ATTITUDE

I hope you took a moment to read the paragraph on attitude by Charles Swindoll on the November introduction page. Read it every day and use its wisdom to anchor your perspective and your attitude for that day. Growth and beauty and joy can only appear in your life when you provide the positive attitude climate.

Life is too good to feel bad.
— **Motrin - TV Advertising Commercial**

Laughter changes our perception of pain; physical and emotional.
— **Dr. Robert Basso**

Onions make people cry but we've not yet discovered
a vegetable that makes people laugh.
— **Will Rogers**

Always have good thoughts: they may break into words at any time.

NOVEMBER 3

TODAY, I find joy in my habit to SHOW A POSITIVE ATTITUDE

Smiles improve our attitudes and make life easier. Smiling stimulates the nervous system to produce "cerebral morphine." This hormone gives us a pleasant feeling and has an anesthetic effect. It also takes fewer calories to smile than frown. It takes 72 muscles to frown and only 14 to smile. When you're feeling "down" you can help lift your spirits with a smile. Call or plan to see a friend who is outgoing and upbeat. Find the light-hearted shows on TV or the internet. Here's one I found - WEBSITE: http://www.laughfactory.com/jokes

> *Start every day off with a smile—and get it over with.*
> — **W.C. Fields, American Actor**

> *Smile! It improves your face value*
> — **Ziggy, Tom Wilson**

Love makes the world go 'round but laughter keeps us from falling off.

HABITS FOR UNITY   Yellow

NOVEMBER 4

TODAY, I find joy in my habit to SHOW A POSITIVE ATTITUDE

Keeping a positive outlook in the face of adversity is easier said than done. This is an area of our lives where our friendship communities can be helpful. The best solution is to reach outward, or inward, for help.

> *If your efforts are sometimes greeted with indifference, don't lose heart— the sun puts on a great show every daybreak, yet most of the people in the audience go on sleeping.*
> — **Mark Teixeria, Baseball**

> *Tis easy enough to be pleasant, when life flows along like a song. But the man worthwhile is smiling, when everything else goes dead wrong.*
> — **Ella Wheeler Wilcox, American Author**

It's better to light one candle than to waste electricity.

NOVEMBER 5

TODAY, I find joy in my habit to SHOW A POSITIVE ATTITUDE

Are you concerned about how people treat one another—especially in public—like when shopping, or sightseeing? When you start to think there's not much civility left in public places, just remember that you can actually help shift attitudes around you with your own attitude. There are people who make cheering up others their mission. It's a great idea—and another good way to make life better for ourselves.

> *If all the good people were clever,*
> *And all clever people were good,*
> *The world would be nicer than ever*
> *We thought that it possibly could.*
> — **Elizabeth Wordsworth, "The Clever and the Good"**

The shortest distance between two people is paved with smiles and laughter.

HABITS FOR UNITY   Yellow

NOVEMBER 6

TODAY, I find joy in my habit to SHOW A POSITIVE ATTITUDE

I've heard it said that "balance is everything." Even though a positive attitude makes life so much easier, there is merit to the idea that some of life's low spots help us appreciate and cherish life's joys.

> *My great hope is to laugh as much as I cry; to get my work done and try to love somebody and have the courage to accept the love in return.*
> — **Maya Angelou, American Poet**

> *What the world really needs is more love and less paperwork.*
> — **Pearl Bailey, American Singer-Actress**

> *All sunshine makes a desert.*
> — **Arab Proverb**

NOVEMBER 7
TODAY, I find joy in my habit to SHOW A POSITIVE ATTITUDE

Showing a positive attitude includes what you "don't" as well as what you "do." One of the worst offenders in the attitude department is gossip.

> *If you are tempted to reveal*
> *A tale someone has told to you*
> *About another, before you speak,*
> *Make it pass three gates of gold:*
> *First, 'Is it true?' Then, 'Is it needful?'*
> *And then "Is it kind?'*
> *And if to reach your lips at last*
> *It passes through these gateways three,*
> *Then you may tell the tale, nor fear*
> *What the result of speech may be.*
> — **Beth Day**

Better to light a candle than to 'light a stick of dynamite.

HABITS FOR UNITY   Yellow

NOVEMBER 8
TODAY, I find joy in my habit to SHOW A POSITIVE ATTITUDE

Victor Frankel survived the Nazi concentration camps and wrote a book entitled, "Man's Search for Meaning." I will always remember the distinction he made between the words, Liberty and Freedom. "Liberty," he said, is the condition of being free from restriction confinement, servitude or forced labor. "Freedom" is the capacity to exercise choice and the right to act, believe or express oneself in the manner of one's own choosing.

> *No one can make you unhappy without your consent.*
> — **Anonymous**

> *It isn't your position that makes you happy or unhappy; it's your disposition.*
> — **Dale Carnegie**

I've learned that even when I have pain, I don't have to be one.

NOVEMBER 9

TODAY, I find joy in my habit to SHOW A POSITIVE ATTITUDE

Laughter is not only good for your attitude it:
Strengthens your immune system
Enhances your cardiovascular flexibility
Increases your spirit quotient
Helps you think more clearly
Puts a twinkle in your eye
Increases your information retention
Replenishes your creative juices,
Pops you out of emotional ruts
Releases and transforms emotional pain
Enhances perspective and reminds you of the bigger picture
Enriches your deeper connection with other people.

   —Amy Goodheart, Teehee.com

HABITS FOR UNITY   **Yellow**

NOVEMBER 10

TODAY, I find joy in my habit to SHOW A POSITIVE ATTITUDE

Love is only four letters but its meanings fill volumes. One synonym for love is the word acceptance. There is also a peacefulness about the idea of acceptance that helps keep a positive attitude. Think today about how well you accept the weaknesses and annoying habits of others.

Rainbows are the apology of angry skies.
   — Sylvia Voirol

Life teaches us to be less harsh with ourselves and with others.
   — Johann Wolfgang Von Goethe, German Playwright

Don't count your chickens—it takes too long.

NOVEMBER 11

TODAY, I find joy in my habit to SHOW A POSITIVE ATTITUDE

The problem is not the problem
The problem is one's attitude about the problem.
   —Jeffrey A. Timmons

Joy is not in things; it is in us.
   —Richard Wagner

I've learned that children and grandparents are natural allies.
   — Adrena - Age 13

The excursion is the same when you go looking for your sorrow,
as when you go looking for your joy.
   —Eudora A. Welty, The Wide Net

The only time the world beats a path to your door –
is when you're in the bathroom.

HABITS FOR UNITY  Yellow

NOVEMBER 12

TODAY, I find joy in my habit to SHOW A POSITIVE ATTITUDE

Enjoying the present moment and looking ahead to the future is
an important key to a positive attitude. Practice this today. What is
beautiful around you right now? What moments are planned today
where you will find joy or fulfillment? Are you going to see an old
friend, work on a project with a coworker, or walk in the park?

Keep your face to the sunshine, and you'll never see the shadows.
   — Debbye Turner, Miss America 1990

Nobody gets to live life backward. Look ahead — that's where
your future lies.
   — Ann Landers, Advice Columnist

It's a long old road, but I know I'm gonna find the end.
   — Bessie Smith, American Gospel Singer

Never put off until tomorrow, what
you should have done yesterday.

NOVEMBER 13

TODAY, I find joy in my habit to SHOW A POSITIVE ATTITUDE

A RECIPE FOR THE BLUES

Here's a recipe to cure the blues which is worth a dozen medical remedies:

> *Take one spoonful of pleasant memories.*
> *Take two spoonfuls of endeavors for the happiness of others.*
> *Take two spoonfuls of forgetfulness of sorrow.*
> *Mix well with a half pint of cheerfulness.*
> *Take a portion of this mixture every hour of the day.*
> — **Frances Willard**

Lead me not into temptation. I can find the way myself.

Never knock on death's door; ring the doorbell and run (he hates that!!)

HABITS FOR UNITY		Yellow

NOVEMBER 14

TODAY, I find joy in my habit to SHOW A POSITIVE ATTITUDE

Being able to laugh at ourselves is a great way to avoid self-importance. I only found two quotes about laughing at yourself, but they're worth a few laughs! If you find some quotes in your own travels, please send them to me. Seeing the humor in our own actions is a great form of self-acceptance and a terrific way to "lighten up."

> *Blessed are they who can laugh at themselves, for they shall never cease to be amused.*
> — **Anonymous**

> *You grow up the day you have your first real laugh at yourself.*
> — **Ethel Barrymore**

> *Laugh at yourself first, before anyone else can.*
> — **Elsa Maxwell**

It's not hard to meet expenses... they're everywhere.

NOVEMBER 15
TODAY, I find joy in my habit to SHOW A POSITIVE ATTITUDE

Keeping a positive attitude during adversity is easier when we remember that we actually do "get through" most tough set-backs. Quite often, something better happens. Some people have lost their jobs – then gone on to find a new job in a direction they wouldn't have dreamed of.

> *The soul would have no rainbow had the eyes no tears.*
> — **John Vance Cheney**

> *The worst thing in your life may contain seeds of the best. When you can see crisis as an opportunity, your life becomes not easier, but more satisfying.*
> — **Joe Kogel**

When you're living on the edge, make sure you're wearing your seatbelt.

HABITS FOR UNITY   Yellow

NOVEMBER 16
TODAY, I find joy in my habit to SHOW A POSITIVE ATTITUDE

Today's positive attitude thought—that a smile enhances appearance more than cosmetics or accessories—could cause a drop in sales for the cosmetics industry. Of course, just when we thought they couldn't possibly figure out how to sell us something to make a smile more beautiful, the teeth whiteners came on the market!

> *There is no cosmetic for beauty like happiness.*
> — **Lady Marguerite Blessington**

> *You're never fully dressed without a smile.*
> — **Martin Charnin, Annie**

If God had wanted me to touch my toes, he would have put them on my knees.

NOVEMBER 17

TODAY, I find joy in my habit to SHOW A POSITIVE ATTITUDE

There are "last ditch effort" situations when a firm and even angry attitude seems to be necessary to get what you need. HOWEVER, many people have gotten into the habit of using anger and intimidation all the time. We learned from Mary Poppins that "a spoonful of sugar makes the medicine go down."

You catch more flies with honey.
— **Anonymous**

Sandwich every piece of criticism between two layers of praise.
— **Mary Kay Ash**

It's nice to work with friendly people. Be one.
— **Author Unknown**

For every action, there is an equal and opposite criticism.

HABITS FOR UNITY   **Yellow**

NOVEMBER 18

TODAY, I find joy in my habit to SHOW A POSITIVE ATTITUDE

If there is any other word that is a synonym for "positive attitude" it is the word "hope." Each is impossible without the other.

Hope is the only good that is common to all men; those who have nothing else possess hope still.
— **Thales**

Hope springs eternal in the human breast.
— **Alexander Pope, British Poet**

Where there is life there is hope.
— **Cicero**

He who loses hope may then part with anything.
— **William Congreve, Author**

The hardness of the butter is proportional to the softness of the bread.

NOVEMBER 19
TODAY, I find joy in my habit to SHOW A POSITIVE ATTITUDE

Many have found inspiration in *The Optimist Creed*. It has been used to help patients recover from illness or to motivate the players on sports teams. Optimist International adopted this creed in 1922. It was originally published in 1912 in a book by Christian D. Larson, who believed that people have powers, which can be successfully mobilized with the proper attitude.

HABITS FOR UNITY   **Yellow**

Show a
P☺sitive
ATTITUDE
in November

THE OPTIMIST CREED
Optimist International® Copyright © 1999

Promise Yourself -

> *To be so strong that nothing can disturb your peace of mind.*
>
> *To talk about health, happiness and prosperity to every person you meet.*
>
> *To make all your friends feel that there is something in them.*
>
> *To look at the sunny side of everything and make your optimism come true.*
>
> *To think only of the best, to work only for the best and to expect only the best.*
>
> *To be as enthusiastic about the success of others as you are about your own.*
>
> *To forget the mistakes of the past and press on to the greater achievements of the future.*
>
> *To wear a cheerful countenance at all times and give every living creature you meet a smile.*
>
> *To give so much time to the improvement of yourself that you have no time to criticize others.*
>
> *To be too large for worry, too noble for anger, too strong for fear, and too happy to permit the presence of trouble.*

A penny saved is not much.

NOVEMBER 20

TODAY, I find joy in my habit to SHOW A POSITIVE ATTITUDE

You have to sniff out joy. Keep your nose to the joy-trail.
— **Buffy Sainte-Marie, Folk Singer**

Aqua-dexterous (adjective)—possessing the ability to turn the bathtub on and off with your toes.
— **Author Unknown**

If you keep following the crowd, one day you will get lost in it.
— **Nitin Namdeo, Author at Succedict**

Early to bed and early to rise is first in the bathroom.
— **Author Unknown**

A bird in the hand is a real mess.
— **Author Unknown**

HABITS FOR UNITY   **Yellow**

NOVEMBER 21

TODAY, I find joy in my habit to SHOW A POSITIVE ATTITUDE

One Hug - The Universal Rx.
No moving parts, no batteries.
No monthly payments and no fees;
Inflation-proof, non-taxable,
In fact, it's quite relaxable;
It can't be stolen, won't pollute,
One size fits all, do not dilute;
It uses little energy,
But yields results enormously.
Relieves your tension and your stress,
Invigorates your happiness;
Combats depression, makes you beam,
And elevates your self-esteem!
Your circulation it corrects,
Without unpleasant side effects;
It is, I think, the perfect drug,
May I prescribe, my friend, the hug!
(and, of course, fully returnable!)

NOVEMBER 22

TODAY, I find joy in my habit to SHOW A POSITIVE ATTITUDE

Worrying is sometimes like having a bulldog on the end of a rag—
you can't shake it loose no how.

*Blessed is the person who is too busy to worry in the daytime
and too sleepy to worry at night.*
— **Leo Aikman**

*What's the use of worrying? It never was worthwhile, So, pack
up your troubles in your old kit-bag, and, smile, smile, smile.*
— **George Asaf (George H. Powell)**

*Occupy your minds with good thoughts, or the enemy will fill
them with bad ones.*
— **St. Thomas More**

It's always darkest just before
I open my eyes.

HABITS FOR UNITY   Yellow

NOVEMBER 23

TODAY, I find joy in my habit to SHOW A POSITIVE ATTITUDE

Blessings are the antithesis of worries. November is when we celebrate our blessings with Thanksgiving. Oprah Winfrey suggests
keeping your mind on blessings instead of worries, keep a "Grateful Journal" near your bedside. Every night before going to sleep
write down in the Journal at least five blessings that day that you
are grateful for.

Blessings brighten while we count them.
— **Maltbie D. Babcock**

*Better to lose count while naming your blessings than to lose
your blessings by counting your troubles.*
— **Maltbie D. Babcock**

*Not what we say about our blessings but how we use them is
the true measure of our thanksgiving.*
— **W.T. Purkiser**

Bees hum because they don't know the words.

NOVEMBER 24

TODAY, I find joy in my habit to SHOW A POSITIVE ATTITUDE

> *A positive attitude may not solve your problems, but it will annoy enough people to make it worth the effort.*
> — **Herm Albright**

> *The best way to pay for a lovely moment is to enjoy it.*
> — **Richard Bach, Author**

> *If mom's not happy, nobody's happy.*
> — **Jennifer Neely, Age 13**

> *If you are happy, you can always learn to dance.*
> — **Balinese Saying**

If you can't stand the heat—go swimming.

HABITS FOR UNITY   Show a P☺sitive ATTITUDE *in November*   **Yellow**

NOVEMBER 25

TODAY, I find joy in my habit to SHOW A POSITIVE ATTITUDE

In this overly busy world we share, it's too easy to become too serious about everything. Our "forgotten youth" and its merriment gets lost in the conservative effort to be an "adult." There's a great phrase for this—"Lighten UP!!"

> *Destroy your conservative reputation, laugh uproariously today.*
> — **Danny Kaye**

> *Everybody's got a laughing place.*
> *Trouble is... most folks won't take time to go look for it!*
> — *Briar Rabbit, Character of Robb Sagendorph*

> *The most wasted day of all is that*
> *on which we have not laughed.*
> — **Sebastien Roch Nicolas Chamfort**

Don't waste today. Laugh, and the world will laugh with you.

NOVEMBER 26
TODAY, I find joy in my habit to SHOW A POSITIVE ATTITUDE

A SMILE

Smiling is infectious, you catch it like the flu,
When someone smiled at me today, I started smiling too.

I passed around the corner, and someone saw my grin -
When he smiled, I realized, I'd passed it on to him.

I thought about that smile, then I realized its worth,
A single smile, just like mine, could travel round the earth.

So, if you feel a smile begin, don't leave it undetected -
Let's start an epidemic quick and get the world infected!
   —Wisdom found anonymously on the internet

Smile, and the world smiles with you.
   — Jack Ellison

HABITS FOR UNITY   Yellow

NOVEMBER 27
TODAY, I find joy in my habit to SHOW A POSITIVE ATTITUDE

Here are some more uplifting quotes about smiles.

A warm smile is the universal language of kindness.
   — William Arthur Ward, "Reward Yourself"

Smiles are the soul's kisses.
   — Minna Antrim

Most smiles are started by another smile.
   — Anonymous

Everyone smiles in the same language.
   — Anonymous

A smile is the beginning of peace.
   — Mother Teresa

I've learned that to cheer yourself up,
it's best to try and cheer someone else up.

NOVEMBER 28

TODAY, I find joy in my habit to SHOW A POSITIVE ATTITUDE

Life goes at such a fast pace and we get so caught up in our own affairs that it's easy to forget to really care about others. It's an odd thing to say, but if you think about it, it is often true. This is what happens when we are not listening to another person because we are thinking about what our own response will be. Try expanding your life in a healthy way by jumping into the point of view of someone else today.

You can make your world so much larger
simply by acknowledging everyone else's.
— Jeanne Marie Laskas

A Rolling Stone plays the guitar.

HABITS FOR UNITY Show a P☺sitive ATTITUDE *in November* **Yellow**

NOVEMBER 29

TODAY, I find joy in my habit to SHOW A POSITIVE ATTITUDE

Mary Poppins popularized the "spoonful of sugar" approach to encouraging others. When you want someone in your life to change, there are many ways to work on it. Many people use anger and never realize that anger rarely causes inspired positive changes in anyone.

A pat on the back is only a few inches away from a kick
in the pants, but it is miles ahead in getting results.
— V. Wilcox

You can't give people pride, but you can provide the kind of
understanding that makes people look to their inner strengths
and find their own sense of pride.
— Charleszetta Waddles, Detroit Activist

Two men look out through the same bars;
One sees mud and one the stars.
— Frederick Langbridge

The squeaking wheel gets annoying.

NOVEMBER 30
TODAY, I find joy in my habit to SHOW A POSITIVE ATTITUDE

Sometimes it doesn't make sense to suggest that we have to practice having a positive attitude. We practice everything else, from the multiplication tables to triceps lifts on the weight bar. I have read studies that say people have actually "learned" to become more optimistic. Make an effort from now on to check out your thinking when you get on a negative jag. Practice having a positive thought about the person or event that is getting you down.

> *Happiness is a thing to be practiced, like the violin.*
> — John Lubbock

> *Things turn out the best for people who make the best of the way things turn out.*
> — Art Linkletter

HABITS FOR UNITY  Yellow

Let's close out November on a jovial note. Here are a few more quotes about laughter. With the holiday season ahead, you'll be glad you worked on practicing a positive attitude in November.

> *It is bad to hold back laughter. It goes back down inside and spreads to your hips.*
> — Fred Allen

> *Laughter… the most civilized music in the world*
> — Sir Peter Ustinov, British Actor

December is Month 12

CELEBRATE COMMUNITY, FAMILY AND FRIENDS

*IN **DECEMBER**... and all year long...*

Color Cue — EVER-Green

Health Focus — Healthy Hearts, Minds and Bodies

Affirmation – I love my habit to
CELEBRATE COMMUNITY, FAMILY AND FRIENDS.

"Together we heal the country we all share."

– Elaine Parke

In DECEMBER, REMEMBER TO...
CELEBRATE COMMUNITY, FAMILY AND FRIENDS

December is the last month of the calendar year. This great month of holidays gives me a chance to celebrate you - my readers and friends. December's celebration color is EVER-Green. When I see an evergreen tree, I am reminded of the constancy of relationships throughout our lives.

Evergreen renews and restores depleted energy. It is the sanctuary away from the stresses of modern living, restoring us back to a sense of well-being. We are reminded that it is family and friends and community that are the abiding and enduring aspects of a fulfilling life. Practicing this Unity Habit is a way to keep it all together during the rough spots.

Whether finely-seamed or tattered and torn, relationships are the fabric threads that connect us to one another. "Celebrate Community, Family and Friends" wraps up the year and captures the essence of what the holiday season is all about, no matter what religious or humanistic belief you hold.

December is a time of celebrations when that warm feeling of peace on earth is the strongest. The famous historian Will Durant once said, "Civilization is just the slow process of learning to be kind." I guess the question then is—just how well have we learned to be kind? Imagine how we will feel one day—when peace on earth really comes true. Imagine no violence, no child abuse, no poverty, no hunger, and no war. Cherish kindness. Celebrate your relationships with others this month. Use your 1,440 minutes each day to let them know you care.

Goal for December:
Let there be peace on earth and let it begin with me.

"Together we heal the world we all share."
— **Elaine Parke, Author**

*We tried so hard to make things better for our kids that
we might have made them worse. For my grandchildren,
I'd like better.*

*I'd really like for them to know about hand-me down clothes
and homemade ice cream and leftover meatloaf sandwiches.
I really would.*

*I hope they learn humility by being humiliated, and learn honesty by being cheated. I hope they learn to make their beds and
mow the lawn and wash the car.*

*And, my cherished grand-child, I really hope nobody gives you a
brand-new car when you are sixteen. I hope you have a job
by then.*

*It will be good if at least one time you can see a baby calf born
and your old dog put to sleep.*

*I hope you have to share a bedroom with your younger brother.
And it's alright if you have to draw a line down the middle of the
room, but when he wants to crawl under the covers with you
because he's scared, I hope you let him.*

*When you want to see a Disney movie and your little brother
wants to tag along, I hope you'll let him.*

*I hope you have to walk uphill to school with your friends and
that you live in a town where you can do it safely.*

I hope you learn to dig in the dirt and read books.

*When you learn to use those newfangled computers,
I hope you also learn to add and subtract in your head.*

*I hope you get razzed by your friends when you have your first
crush on a girl, and when you talk back to your mother that you
learn what Ivory soap tastes like.*

*May you skin your knee climbing a mountain, burn your hand
on a stove and get your tongue stuck on a frozen flagpole.*

I sure hope you make time to sit on a porch with your grandpa and go fishing with your uncle. May you feel sorrow at a funeral and the joy of holidays.

I hope your mother punishes you when you throw a baseball through a neighbor's window and that she hugs you and kisses you at holiday time when you give her a plaster of Paris mold of your hand.

These things I wish for you - tough times and disappointment, hard work and above all, happiness.

— Written with a pen........ by Paul Harvey (1918–2009)

Handmade posters done at a "Statewide Teachers" Training Workshop in
Fairmount, WV

DECEMBER 1

TODAY... I love my habit to CELEBRATE
COMMUNITY, FAMILY AND FRIENDS

Start this month with thoughts that focus on your family. Take an audit. How is your marriage, your parenting, your sibling relationships and your own role as the child? Where can you do better? How might you change your priorities?

> *Other things may change us, but we start and end*
> *with the family.*
>
> — **Anthony Brandt**

> *To us, family means putting your arms around each other and*
> *being there.*
>
> —**Barbara Bush, former First Lady**

CELEBRATE: A renewal of family

HABITS FOR UNITY   Green

DECEMBER 2

TODAY... I love my habit to CELEBRATE
COMMUNITY, FAMILY AND FRIENDS

I heard a joke the other day - that what most people make best for dinner these days is reservations. We live in a fast-paced society. It's way too easy to get on the fast track with no time to share food at home ourselves. Step down off the track today, especially if you are a parent. How's your "loving involvement" doing? What will you change?

> *Home cooking is something a lot of families are not.*
>
> — **Anonymous**

> *A sense of belonging, the loving involvement of parents which*
> *creates a sense of worth, and a sense of purpose - are what ev-*
> *ery child deserves to receive.*
>
> — **Cyril J. Barber**

CELEBRATE: Prepare a meal and eat together at home tonight.

DECEMBER 3

TODAY... I love my habit to CELEBRATE
COMMUNITY, FAMILY AND FRIENDS

Focus on spending time with loved ones.

> *The best inheritance a parent can give his children is a few min-*
> *utes of his time each day.*
> — O.A. Battista

> *Spare the rod and spoil the child—that is true. But besides the*
> *rod, keep an apple to give him when he has done well.*
> — Martin Luther, German Theologian

CELEBRATE: Think about the best family
meal you can remember. Was it
because the food was good?

HABITS FOR UNITY   Green

DECEMBER 4

TODAY... I love my habit to CELEBRATE
COMMUNITY, FAMILY AND FRIENDS

Examine the question, "How do you make a habit out of loving relationships?" What is the quality of "more than friendship?"

> *Mummy herself has told us that she looked upon us more as her*
> *friends than her daughters. Now that is all very fine, but still, a*
> *friend can't take a mother's place. I need my mother as an ex-*
> *ample which I can follow. I want to be able to respect her.*
> — Anne Frank, The Diary of a Young Girl

> *One has to grow up with good talk in order to form*
> *the habit of it.*
> — Helen Hayes, American Actress

CELEBRATE: Spend an hour listening.

DECEMBER 5

TODAY... I love my habit to CELEBRATE
COMMUNITY, FAMILY AND FRIENDS

Setting a good example for children is a win-win effort. Exemplary behavior improves our own lives and sense of self-worth too. We know children are astonishingly perceptive. Parenting "How-To" courses won't help us to create healthy well-adjusted children unless we show children good examples in our own lives. I call it "being our best-self."

> *A child is not likely to find a father in God until he finds something of God in his father.*
> — Austin L. Sorensen

> *Children don't want to be told; they want to be shown. It takes years of telling to undo one unwise showing.*
> — Eileen M. Haase, Professor

CELEBRATE: Show someone your "best self" today.

HABITS FOR UNITY		Green

DECEMBER 6

TODAY... I love my habit to CELEBRATE
COMMUNITY, FAMILY AND FRIENDS

Mutual respect is the essence of the Golden Rule. I also think mutual respect is the essence of good parenting. All too often respect for a child's dignity and worth gets lost in our outbursts of anger and criticism.

> *It is etiquette for a son or daughter to talk to the father in a gentle and polite tone, and the parent, except when reprimanding or correcting his children, is required by custom to reciprocate the compliment in the same way as his children extend it to him.*
> — Jomo Kenyatta, On Gikuyu (Central Kenya) Custom

CELEBRATE: The dignity of children. Balance criticism with praise.

DECEMBER 7

*TODAY... I love my habit to CELEBRATE
COMMUNITY, FAMILY AND FRIENDS*

My own childhood was like "trying to grow up in the display window of a furniture store." My mom had a Bachelor of Science in Home Economics and not one mess was ever allowed—anywhere in the house at all—period. When I saw this quote by Phyllis Diller, I called mom immediately and said, "Here's one for you!"

Cleaning your house while your kids are still growing is like shoveling the walk before it stops snowing.

— **Phyllis Diller, Actress-Comedienne**

CELEBRATE: Make a big mess.

HABITS FOR UNITY   Green

DECEMBER 8

*TODAY... I love my habit to CELEBRATE
COMMUNITY, FAMILY AND FRIENDS*

Another quality, too often lost in today's fast-paced world, is that of AWE and our sense of the sacred. Look into the face of a child. Know you are looking at the miracle of creation and our hope for the future of the world.

Every child comes with the message that God is not yet discouraged of man (woman).

— **Rabindranath Tagore, Stray Birds**

CELEBRATE: Tuck someone into bed tonight.

DECEMBER 9

TODAY... I love my habit to CELEBRATE
COMMUNITY, FAMILY AND FRIENDS

Our family is our own personal "hardy" EVER-green. Its shape or form doesn't matter. Whether our family is a nuclear unit, an extended step-family, blood related, adopted or by choice... once formed, with love, family weathers any storm.

> *The family is a community of persons and the smallest social unit. It is the cradle of life and love, the place in which the individual "is born" and "grows."*
> — **Pope John Paul II, "Letter to Families"**

> *Family faces are magic mirrors. Looking at people who belong to us, we see the* past, present and future.
> — **Gail Lumet Buckley**

CELEBRATE: Remember and cherish
your most recent hug.

HABITS FOR UNITY   **Green**

DECEMBER 10

TODAY... I love my habit to CELEBRATE
COMMUNITY, FAMILY AND FRIENDS

> *Home is the place where, when you have to go there,*
> *they have to take you in.*
> — **Robert Frost, American Poet**

> *In prosperity, our friends know us; in adversity, we know our friends.*
> — **John Churton Collins, Literary critic**

CELEBRATE: The meaning of home.

DECEMBER 11

TODAY... I love my habit to CELEBRATE
COMMUNITY, FAMILY AND FRIENDS

What is important to you about being a parent? You have probably heard the saying that "We owe our children only roots and wings." Sometimes, we forget that the heritage of our earth is part of what we owe our children. Clean air and water and a thriving ecosystem are the only ways to insure their passage into a healthy future.

> *We have not inherited the earth from our ancestors;*
> *we are borrowing it from our children.*
> — **Anonymous**

> *Every child born into this world belongs to the whole human race.*
> — **Greer Garson, Irish Actress**

CELEBRATE: Make the earth a part of
December's celebration.
Recycle or walk instead of drive.

HABITS FOR UNITY · **Celebrate COMMUNITY, FAMILY & FRIENDS in December** · Green

DECEMBER 12

TODAY... I love my habit to CELEBRATE
COMMUNITY, FAMILY AND FRIENDS

Friendship is as old as society itself. Cicero was a great Roman philosopher, orator and statesman. Two thousand years ago, in letters to his brother and friends, he shared with them—and with us—the philosophy of stoicism and life that we still know today.

> *Friendship adds a brighter radiance to prosperity and lightens the burden of adversity by dividing and sharing it.*
> — **Cicero**

> *Friendship is nothing else than an accord in all things, human and divine, enjoined with mutual good will and affection, and I am inclined to think that, with the exception of wisdom, no better thing has been given to man.*
> — **Cicero**

CELEBRATE: Write a letter to a friend.

DECEMBER 13

*TODAY... I love my habit to CELEBRATE
COMMUNITY, FAMILY AND FRIENDS*

It's the holiday season and a time when stress can build up and cause friction between family and friends. The holidays are about joyfulness, not about having too much to do. As the old saying goes, "Keep your eye on the donut, not the hole." Keep your eyes on the people you love and not the stuff, even if the stuff is the gifts you are buying for those you love. Remember that the true gift is YOU.

Fair or foul weather, we must all stick together.
   — Underdog, "Underdog"

Treat your friends as you do your pictures, and place them in the best possible light.
   — Jennie Jerome Churchill, "Friendship"

CELEBRATE: Put people ahead of stuff.

HABITS FOR UNITY   Green

DECEMBER 14

*TODAY... I love my habit to CELEBRATE
COMMUNITY, FAMILY AND FRIENDS*

Make two lists this holiday season. One list is the gifts you will give and the other is the visits you plan to make to the homes of family and friends and perhaps to a senior home or a volunteer center. Once you have made your lists, begin the joyous journey of planning the time to do it.

Go oft to the house of thy friend,
for weeds choke the unused path.
   — Ralph Waldo Emerson, Author, Poet and Essayist

Fate chooses our relatives; we choose our friends.
   — Jacques Delillie, Poet

CELEBRATE: Take time to visit a friend.

DECEMBER 15
TODAY... I love my habit to CELEBRATE
COMMUNITY, FAMILY AND FRIENDS

My friends are my wealth.
> — Emily Dickinson, Poet

I never met a man (person) I didn't like.
> — Will Rogers, American Humorist

Don't walk in front of me... I may not follow.
Don't walk behind me... I may not lead.
Walk beside me... just be my friend.
> —Albert Camus

CELEBRATE: The wealth you chose
for yourself.

HABITS FOR UNITY   Green

DECEMBER 16
TODAY... I love my habit to CELEBRATE
COMMUNITY, FAMILY AND FRIENDS

What is friendship? We all have friendships that ebb and flow - sometimes we see friends frequently and sometimes months pass with
no contact. We call them friends, because we know that they can be
counted on to be there for us (and vice versa) if needed. That's why
I've often thought that the difference between a "fair weather friend"
and a "foul weather friend" is much more than the weather.

A true friend is someone who is there for you when he'd rather
be somewhere else.
> — Len Wein

A friend in need is a friend indeed.
> — Quintus Ennius

CELEBRATE: Give up something to be there for a friend.

DECEMBER 17

TODAY… I love my habit to CELEBRATE
COMMUNITY, FAMILY AND FRIENDS

As you go through your day, in meetings, at your desk or work-station, in classrooms, family rooms and the grocery store, look around you. Every person you see is a friend or family member somewhere - to someone - and every person is part of the meaning in the lives of one another.

> *Friendship is the only cement that will hold the world together.*
> **— Duke Ellington, American Musician**

> *How rare and wonderful is that flash of a moment when we realize we have discovered a friend.*
> **— William Rotsler, American artist**

CELEBRATE: Appreciate the friends we already know and those we are about to discover.

HABITS FOR UNITY   **Green**

DECEMBER 18

TODAY… I love my habit to CELEBRATE
COMMUNITY, FAMILY AND FRIENDS

If you own a pet, or have walked down the pet aisle at the grocery store recently, then you probably understand that pets give us something we need. They give us the kind of unquestionable, totally accepting love that we yearn for in our relationships with people. If there were a synonym for love I would suggest the word "acceptance."

> *We give them the love we can spare the time we can spare. In return, dogs have given us their absolute all. It is without a doubt the best deal man has ever made.*
> **— Roger Caras, Pres. A.S.P.C.A.**

CELEBRATE: Acceptance as your definition for love.

DECEMBER 19
TODAY... I love my habit to CELEBRATE
COMMUNITY, FAMILY AND FRIENDS

Just say, "I'll be there." Being there for a friend is the greatest gift we can give. When we help others, healthy things happen to them and to us. We are renewed in love and our spirits soar.

> *When you face a crisis, you know who your true friends are.*
> — **Earvin "Magic" Johnson, Los Angeles Lakers**

> *Winter, spring, summer or fall*
> *All you have to do is call*
> *And I'll be there*
> *You've got a friend.*
> — **Carole King, American Singer-Composer**

CELEBRATE: Practice saying,
"I'll be there."

HABITS FOR UNITY	Green

DECEMBER 20
TODAY... I love my habit to CELEBRATE
COMMUNITY, FAMILY AND FRIENDS

Are you a "masterpiece" friend and a "garden of delight?" We all grow up with our garden of weeds; a short temper, impatience with others, a tendency to self-absorption, an inability to listen— we each have our own embarrassing list. But as we become more aware of our weeds, and how they affect others, we can prune the thorns, cut the dead wood and clear and plant the seeds of consideration and compassion.

> *An old friend can be a garden of true delight.*
> — **Nick Beilenson**

> *A friend may well be reckoned the masterpiece of nature.*
> — **Ralph Waldo Emerson, Poet, Author and Essayist**

CELEBRATE: Pick a fault (like not listening) and
start hacking away at it!

DECEMBER 21

TODAY... I love my habit to CELEBRATE
COMMUNITY, FAMILY AND FRIENDS

This is the time of year when peace and love are in the air. It's a good time to grab a hold of the spirit of love and make a resolution to keep it going.

> *It is change that makes the world go round — but its love that keeps it populated.*
> **— Charles H. Brower**

> *Everything in the household runs smoothly when love oils the machinery.*
> **— William H. (Rosy) Grier**

CELEBRATE: The spirit of peace and love. This month we celebrate Hanukkah. Read the story of why this holiday is one of light and of dedication.

HABITS FOR UNITY	Celebrate COMMUNITY, FAMILY & FRIENDS in December	Green

DECEMBER 22

TODAY... I love my habit to CELEBRATE
COMMUNITY, FAMILY AND FRIENDS

A man who was moving to Athens asked Socrates what the Athenian people were like. Socrates asked him what people were like in his own town and the man replied that they were selfish and mean. Socrates said, "That too, is just the kind of people you will find in Athens."

Later, another traveler asked Socrates what the people were like in Athens. Socrates queried him about the people in his own home town and the traveler said he missed his home full of neighbors and friends who cared for one another. Socrates then said, "Well that's just the kind of people you will find on your way through our beautiful city of Athens."

> *'Tis the people, not the houses that makes the city.*
> **— Thomas Fuller**

CELEBRATE: Knowing that your own attitude is the key.

DECEMBER 23
TODAY... I love my habit to CELEBRATE
COMMUNITY, FAMILY AND FRIENDS

The most important thing every parent can do for their children is to love and/or respect one another. Teaching children the meaning of healthy love and doing it by example is critical to their growth and development. It also is a true celebration of life.

> *The most important thing a father can do for his children is to love their mother.*
> — **Rev. Theodore M. Hesburgh, Notre Dame**

CELEBRATE: Have a "date" with
your loved-one today.

HABITS FOR UNITY   Green

DECEMBER 24
TODAY... I love my habit to CELEBRATE
COMMUNITY, FAMILY AND FRIENDS

Do you remember the beginning of December and our quote from the famous historian Will Durant? He said, "Civilization is just the slow process of learning to be kind." This month of December has been a slow process of reminders about the kindness of parenting, family, friendships and love. When we focus on what's really essential—life starts to become very simple—not necessarily easy—but simple.

> *It's no use trying to be clever—we are all clever here;*
> *just try to be kind—a little kind.*
> — **F.J. Foakes Jackson**

> *Kind words can be short and easy to speak,*
> *but their echoes are truly endless.*
> — **Mother Teresa, Missionaries of Charity**

CELEBRATE: The simplicity of kindness.

DECEMBER 25

*TODAY... I love my habit to CELEBRATE
COMMUNITY, FAMILY AND FRIENDS*

Today Christians celebrate the birthday of a Son and a man of love,
Jesus Christ.

> *The unity that binds us all together, that makes this earth
> a family, and all men brothers and the sons of God, is love.*
> — **Thomas Wolfe, American Author**

> *There is no surprise more magical than the surprise of being
> loved. It is the finger of God on one's shoulder.*
> — **Charles Morgan**

CELEBRATE: The abundance of love in the world.

HABITS FOR UNITY   Green

DECEMBER 26

*TODAY... I love my habit to CELEBRATE
COMMUNITY, FAMILY AND FRIENDS*

> *As man increased his knowledge of the heavens, why should he
> fear the unknown on earth? As man draws nearer to the stars,
> why should he not also draw nearer to his neighbor?*
> — **Lyndon B. Johnson, 36th President of the US**

> *The world must be narrowed to a neighborhood before it can
> broaden to a brotherhood.*
> — **Lyndon B. Johnson, 36th President of the US**

CELEBRATE: Let there be peace on earth, and let it begin with me.

DECEMBER 27
TODO... I love my habit to CELEBRATE
COMMUNITY, FAMILY AND FRIENDS

Sometimes I scratch my head and chuckle at all of us—like gerbils in a wheel—chasing the illusive something or other. I saw a satirical cartoon in the newspaper that defined the new American Dream as "Me, Mine... Money." Our shared truth that we all have known—all along—is that it is love, not love of money that makes us happy. Love is not only free—it doesn't even exist unless you give it away.

> *To love others makes us happy.*
>   — **Kenny "Babyface" Edmonds, Composer**

> *The love you give away is the only love you keep.*
>   — **Elbert Hubbard**

> *Love is the glue that holds friendships together.*
>   — **Antonio "L.A." Reid, American Composer**

CELEBRATE: LOVE.

HABITS FOR UNITY   **Green**

Celebrate COMMUNITY, FAMILY & FRIENDS in December

DECEMBER 28
TODAY... I love my habit to CELEBRATE
COMMUNITY, FAMILY AND FRIENDS

Sometimes, holidays can feel even more lonely than the rest of the year. There's a heightened sense of the "ideal family" that surrounds us - on TV and during the course of festivities and family gatherings. We may think that our lives and family are not like that. When our actual experience seems to fall short of this ideal, it feels like something that should be there is missing. Remember, that there is no IDEAL for love or family—there are moments of fullness and moments of emptiness in all lives.

> *Love makes the lonelies go away.*
>   — **Ziggy, Tom Wilson**

> *Love is two people...patiently feeding each other,*
> *not one living through the soul of the other.*
>   — **Bessie Head**

CELEBRATE: The ever-present and surprising simplicity of love.

DECEMBER 29

TODAY... I love my habit to CELEBRATE
COMMUNITY, FAMILY AND FRIENDS

Once in a while in life, we find the need to look for new friends and a new sense of community. Perhaps you are single, and have just been transferred to a new town. Perhaps you just couldn't travel back to old roots to share the holidays. One of the best ways to make new friends is to join together in giving. Participate with "friends to be" at the Salvation Army or with Habitat for Humanity or with a local food bank or community outreach.

> *There is always something left to love.*
> *And if you ain't learned that, you ain't learned nothing.*
> — **Lorraine Hansberry, American Playwright**

CELEBRATE: The camaraderie of giving.

HABITS FOR UNITY   Celebrate COMMUNITY, FAMILY & FRIENDS in December   **Green**

DECEMBER 30

TODAY... I love my habit to CELEBRATE
COMMUNITY, FAMILY AND FRIENDS

In the midst of the holiday festivities, take time to reflect on our larger purpose. Do you believe, as I do, that every one of us is here to fulfill our own purpose in the Larger Plan of Human Brother/Sisterhood? While replacing a light bulb, have you ever lost one of the screws that holds the light fixture together? To me, the idea that even one person doesn't count is absurd! Let there be peace on earth, and let it begin with me.

> *Human brotherhood is not just a goal. It is a condition on*
> *which our way of life depends. Our question is whether we*
> *have the strength and the will to make the brotherhood of*
> *man the guiding principle of our daily lives.*
> — **John F. Kennedy, 35th President of the US**

CELEBRATE: Our place in the world.

DECEMBER 31
TODAY... I love my habit to CELEBRATE
COMMUNITY, FAMILY AND FRIENDS

Tonight, we will celebrate New Year's Eve. Of all the days of the year, this day is when the future is a great part of our awareness. What are your New Year's Resolutions? How many are about family, friends and neighbors and how many are about professional success and material goals?

> *An optimist stays up until midnight to see the New Year in.*
> *A pessimist stays up to make sure the old year leaves.*
> — **Bill Vaughn, Actor**

HABITS FOR UNITY	Green

Out with the old, in with the new...
is a fitting expression for a holiday that is based on vomiting.
> — **Andy Borowitz, Writer, Comedian**

Don't make resolutions without an action plan.
The secret to success is right in your hands.
> — **J. Allen Shaw, Poet**

Cheers to a new year and another chance to get it right.
> — **Oprah Winfrey**

It's never too late to be what you might have been.
> — **George Eliot,**
>   **pen name for English Novelist, Mary Ann Evans**

You know how I dread the whole year.
Well this year I'm only going to dread one day at a time.
> — **Charlie Brown – Creator, Charles Schulz**

CELEBRATE: The New Year with love and respect for every one of your fellow men/women.

CONCLUSION AND NEW BEGINNINGS

"Do as you will, but harm no one.
What you give will be returned to you threefold."
    – Alice Hoffman, *Magic Lessons*

This is NOT the end of this book. It may be 365 days later than the day you purchased it or received it from a friend or family member. However, it is NOT the end of *The Habits of Unity* for you or the end of the becoming unity movement for all of us… all across America.

This is why. We have been buying Ford automobiles for 120 years and McDonald's fast foods for 80 years. If we keep investing our time and creativity in repeating and reminding ourselves of the 12 unifying monthly habits the way corporations remind us of their products – Becoming Unity in America will grow. Hopefully, together, we will create a level playing field for the power of unity to help heal the stressful divisiveness that has had such a hold on our nation.

The end of this book, therefore, is a BEGINNING, not an end. The story didn't end with what you just read. The story is the new adventures you are going to live and enjoy in your life from now on. Just like all holidays return every year, together, day after day, month after month, year after year, we can celebrate each colorful habit again and again. The monthly habits can return every year to your life and to the lives of us all. Let us re-discover the sense of awe and sacred wonder that childhood still holds for us each day.

"Life is the childhood of our immortality."
    – Goerthe

The Habits of Unity was prepared for you as a simple, practical book about what a fulfilled and enriched way of life has always meant to me. It has been my hope to bring readers back to the "forgotten shreds of simplicity in our quiet hearts." It is a new chapter in the RALLY of our shared human spirit that is bursting to be set free.

This is a RALLY that unifies us around what we have in common - the need to give and to receive love, appreciation and respect. For me, the goal is to forever change us from humans into humanes. Humanes are people who are actually living their lives with the connecting empathy for one another that has gotten lost in the tangled snarl of technology and money.

The future of *The Habits of Unity: 12 Months to a Stronger America* will be written, not by Elaine Parke, but by you. Please share your stories about how and what you are doing in your own life, with your family and in your community. Post your ideas for making your own colorful habit-building reminders. Write monthly themed music, raps, poetry, stories and drama or create artwork to symbolize these 12 qualities, one colorful month at a time. Post them on your social networks and send them to www.12habits4allofus.org.

Let's rediscover the common purpose that the United States of America was founded to uphold, however imperfectly we have lived it so far. Think about what life will be like when the 12 habits of a more unified America become powerful beyond measure. The possibilities are endless:

> Our own lives will be enriched beyond measure.
>
> Our marriages or committed relationships will be strengthened.
>
> Our families will be stronger and happier.
>
> Our children will thrive.
>
> Our work environment will be a joy and a place of personal fulfillment.
>
> Productivity will multiply as inter-personal problems diminish.
>
> Our earth will be valued as the one thing we all share.
>
> Air and water will be cleaner, there will be less litter, and less waste.
>
> There will be fewer hungry people – or people without homes.

There will be fewer fights and fewer wars.

There will be more smiles.

There will be fewer frowns.

There will be more peace and tranquility.

And..

And...

The possibilities are endless.

Before concluding this writing, I want to share one more personal story.

Since I began this "good habit-building" journey in 1987, I have met many fabulous and interesting people, young and old, across the country and internationally. However, I will never forget one Professor at Carnegie Mellon University in Pittsburgh, Pennsylvania. He inquired about my (then) school project, The Caring Habit of the Month Adventure.

I explained to him my 12-month habit-building concept with my usual three points; (1) everything will get better if we all treated each other better, (2) the repetitive principles of media are powerful, habit-forming and they reach everyone, (3) each person is important and our daily actions have more influence on life than we realize.

Finally, when I paused for a few moments to catch my breath, I noticed a twinkle in his eye as he folded his arms over his well-rounded belly and looked down over his smudged professorial half-glasses to see me better. Then he said,

"Let me see if I understand you, Elaine. You want everyone to be nicer to each other ---- so you're just going to keep pestering us until we start doing it."

Yes, I am guilty of wanting to "pester all of us" until more of us practice kindness and compassion more often than ever before. Rarely, have I been blessed with a better opportunity to chuckle at myself. Thank you, Professor Baumann, wherever you are.

The first "All of Us Flag" was designed and created in 1992 by textile artist, Connie Flaugher, a talented life-long friend of Elaine Parke. One of these flags was presented, by the author, to the, then, Director of the Rwandan National Unity and Reconciliation Commission (NURC) in October of 2006.

Thank you, readers, for joining with me in this *The Habits of Unity* adventure. I hope your new beginning has been joyous and fulfilling and will continue on into your life. I would love to hear your stories about your adventures and events that have happened to you because of the new improved journey you are on. Just visit and add your comments on our website, **www.12habits4allofus.org**.

Remember, to keep the 12 habits going in your life. You can keep reading the one-minute motivations daily, year after year. It is not meant to end. Ever.

ABOUT THE AUTHOR

Author with her wolf friend Logan. Logan visited Berkeley Springs, as a part of a 12 habits March program for the ideal to, "Resolve Conflicts." Wolf "Educators" gave a program on the habitats of wolves and the fact that they often get along better in their own "packs" than people do.

Elaine Parke, MBA, CS, CM, NSA

"I am now nice to the people I used to be mean to."

This 2016 survey quote from a 6th grader, sums up the results of Elaine Parke's life, passion, mission, and work.

For 30 years, her scalable and evidence-driven, 12 habits social unity model, has transformed several million community citizens and youth to feel more caring and connected to one another - across the USA's Midwest, and in Rwanda.

Mrs. Parke is an informed and stimulating media guest and speaker who readily shares her stunningly simple, attractive, and grow-able solution to speed our progress toward a sustainable civilization through mutual respect and kindness. In 1993, her monthly-branded and colorful habit-forming model was deemed a "Social Invention" by the London Institute for Social Inventions.

Born in Coshocton, OH, in January of 1942, just a month after Pearl Harbor, Elaine's life spans the post WWII trajectory of the US culture through industrialization and into the transformative technological whirlwind of mass communications and the internet.

"We smugly praise our civilization as technologically advanced. There is, however, a catastrophic price. Society is collapsing under the massive weight of social and economic inequality, racialism, and the power-driven greed of corporate, political, and climate insensitive corruption." – Elaine Parke

In this books introductory section, Parke retells the Cherokee parable of the struggle between the two wolves of good and bad that is always going on inside each of us. This struggle is also raging throughout America and around the world, fueled by the massive growth of technology. The momentum, so far in the 21st century, is feeding the bad wolf of destruction.

Parke is a lifelong youth-volunteer. At age 19, TIME Magazine reported on Elaine's tutoring and mentoring work with Chicago Racketeer, Cobra and Vice-Lord gang kids. Then, a liberal arts student at Northwestern University she asked herself, "How do we expand the scope of positive, connecting, and more humane influence to reach more people more easily?"

First, she spent twenty-five years fine-tuning her mass-market media skills in corporate America. There, her multi-media campaigns for various corporate products reached and motivated the buying behaviors of millions of people with only a small staff.

It was in October of 1987, that Elaine first had a life-changing vision: that the world-wide, and well- known names of the 12 months of the year could become "brand names" for 12 aspects of equitable Golden Rule living, aka the wisdom of the ages.

"Imagine what our country will be like when these monthly unifying action themes become celebrated as "holi-months" and become better known than Coca Cola? Imagine when March is celebrated nationally as the month to RESOLVE CONFLICTS?" – Elaine Parke

By 1994, Elaine Parke had successfully built and piloted a multi-media model in Somerset, PA. There, with university sponsored research, residents reported that because they simultaneously saw and heard the monthly messages throughout the community, they felt more cared about and connected to one another.

In May, 1999, her model was funded by Blue Cross to help what was then one of the worst school districts in Pennsylvania. After just 18 months, the success of the habits' positive influence on students earned Pennsylvania's Violence-Free Youth Governor's Award. Then Governor and Mrs. Tom Ridge became Honorary Chairpersons.

In 2001, Elaine's first book, *"Join the Golden Rule Revolution - Practice One Habit Each month of the Year,"* (now out of print) was published. After a 60-city Waldenbooks publicity and speaking tour, the first edition sold out.

In 2006-07, with support from Rotary International Elaine was sent to post-genocide Rwanda to train educators. 12 Caring Habits Rwanda is helping prevent future genocides by promoting peace among Rwanda's youth. She was awarded a Paul Harris fellow and a Commendation by the Republic of Rwanda and the National Unity and Reconciliation Commission.

In 2013, Elaine moved from Pennsylvania to Berkeley Springs, WV. There a new community-wide model successfully united schools and more than 65 business and organizational "Ambassadors" around the monthly message habits. Once again successful survey results among the population of 18,000, after less than two years, replicated the results in Somerset, PA – nearly twenty years earlier. The annual implementation cost per person was less than 87 cents.

Today, Elaine Parke is a proud member of the West Virginia Public Broadcasting Friends Board of Directors. She is also working with peers, partners and potential liaisons, posting, blogging and speaking out. With this book, *The Habits of Unity*, her goal is to more quickly expand the potential for the monthly habits model to become a unifying counterforce to the dis-eased divisiveness and selfish individualism that is ruining life for all in America. Her life's motto is "Only together will we heal the country we all share."

You can reach Elaine by visiting the website, **12habits4allofus.org**.

ABOUT THE GRAPHIC DESIGNER

Kurt E. Griffith, Fantastic Realities Studio

Kurt is a veteran Art Director, Graphic Designer, and Illustrator. He is a skilled, experienced, and versatile graphics professional with over 40 years of experience.

Kurt has a BFA with honors in Graphic Design and Illustration from the renowned Pratt Institute in Brooklyn, NY. He entered the industry in 1980 B.C. (Before Computers!) in the murky prehistory prior to desktop publishing. He therefore possesses both traditional and digital studio skills and considers himself a battle-scarred veteran of the Desktop Publishing Wars.

Over the successful span of a long and diverse career, Kurt has accumulated skills in Art Direction, Graphic and Web Design, Digital Art, Illustration, Photography, Electronic Publishing, Audio and Video Production, and Design Consulting. His career includes working both independently and as a staff artist; both solo and with creative teams and workgroups.

His creative projects range includes; magazine & book designs, website development, brochures, logos, illustrations, photography, media kits, and audio and video projects. He has even painted totem poles. His broad range of skills and stylistic approaches enable him to execute client's projects from napkin sketch concept to finished production art.

Raised in Brooklyn, NY, he moved to Rockland County, NY in 2001. Leaving corporate service after the 9/11 attacks – Kurt established **Fantastic Realities Studio** as a versatile source for seasoned and professional design solutions. In 2014, he relocated his home and studio to Berkeley Springs, WV, where he continues to practice his craft in the Appalachian foothills. He remains connected to the world via a broadband internet connection.

Kurt is also an accomplished world percussionist, sacred bard, and ceremonial singer. He is a member of the local drum emsemble **Shangö Percusison** and is a faciliatator for **Shenandoah Rhythm Jams**. He supports the **Morgan Arts Council**, and also serves on the Board of Directors of **Four Quarters Interfaith Sanctuary** in Artemas, PA.

You can visit the Fantastic Realities Studo web site at: **www.fantastic-realities.com**

MoonStruck, Editorial Illustration by Kurt Griffith, acrylic on canvas, 1979, restored 2015.

RESEARCH DATA AND PUBLISHED
THEORETICAL WRITINGS BY ELAINE PARKE

The WIN/WIN WHOLE COMMUNITY
The 12 Monthly Habits Containment Circle

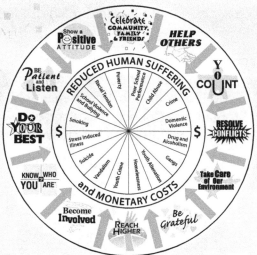

A COMMUNITY CLIMATE
with 12 Habits Motivated Actions

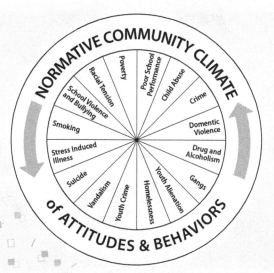

A typical COMMUNITY CLIMATE
without 12 Habits Motivations

Mass Appeal
Expanding the Scope of Positive Influence Beyond the Media

Mass Appeal

Expanding The Scope of Positive Influence Beyond the Media

by Elaine Parke -Founder of Caring Habits

O ur educational system now resides in a complex and fast-paced climate called the information age. Despite the call to come together as community to instill citizenship in our youth, there is a powerful community member that doesn't attend school conferences or sit on community task forces **called the mass media**.

Reprint of article which appeared in The National Association of Secondary School Principals publication - "Schools in the Middle" - November 1999

The media appeal to the young teen group, particularly at the middle level, who often can be resistant to values messages delivered by adults in the classroom or at home. This non-resident can influence youth because they do not perceive the media as authoritarian.

Marshall McLuhan, a Canadian educator in mass communications who probed mass media, wrote in h is 1967 book The Medium Is the Message;

The family circle has widened. The world pool of information fathered by electronic media far surpasses any possible influence mom and dad can now bring to bear. Character no longer is shaped by only two earnest, fumbling experts. Now all the world is the stage.

Mass media have transformed the dynamics of daily living. Adolescents are being taught by the media to think in images and sound bites as a result of spending three minutes per day in dialogue with parents and three hours in front of television or Internet screens. Stability, security, and a sense of caring have been replaced by tension, incivility, and isolation. It's no wonder that students can become morally lost or react with rebellion and violence. Educators and the community

need to build a strategy to engage this powerful non-resident.

Integration is a current educational buzz word. It describes the common use of materials across educational disciplines; or, an integration of social objectives like service learning with educational objectives like math skills or social studies. Integrated educational messages and images, simultaneously delivered, can provoke thought and motivation. For years, educators have been using educational messages as a medium to support learning objectives, but they haven't used media principles to manage the overall influence of the messages. There is a BIG difference. Media can change behaviors and attitudes because when their principles are applied the messages are consistent and repetitive. Otherwise, media are confusing and fragmented. Look around a classroom or take a walk around your school. Write down the three or four main educational messages you see. Are your school's visual messages confusing or consistent? Are there definable visual messages?

Media experts believe it takes six imprints of a single message to embed a thought or idea into long-term memory. Media experts apply repetition and reinforcement techniques that educators use to teach the alphabet or the multiplication tables--

esting point is the suitability of one month frame for one rotation of one message. ists say it takes approximately 21-30 nvert a consistent thought or action into would mean that a school plan or char-

ent ude ent , one nonth ool

cross oday are implementing citizenship and development programs. In most cases, a development program is selected or even veloped internally. This process encourages the enthusiasm and involvement of the stakeholders. Think about character development and citizenship programming in your school.

Now mentally take that walk around your school again. Imagine a single citizenship trait that you want to instill in students, such as Be Responsible. Imagine that the hallways are lined with similar posters all containing variations ot that same message, or with famous quotes, images of famous people, or artwork by students--all focused on the idea to Be Responsible.

With a consistent and rotating messaging plan, classroom walls and hallways will disseminate positive ideas that are consistent and repetitive instead of confusing and fragmented. This can't happen unless there is agreement at a broad level what the consistent plan of messages is. In the 10 years I have been working to integrate media principles into community-building and character education programming. I have discovered that the issue of agreement is the key to successful media integration into education.

1. Do you have a programming in place or plans to adopt a program? What is your process?

2. Can you include a broad area of agreement about curriculum and values messages as one of your goals so expansion and media integration can be facilitated?

3. What are the areas of disagreement that are difficult to overcome?

4. How important are the reasons for different perspectives?

5. Can the disagreements be overcome for the sake of strengthening your program's influence on our youth?

6. How can you broaden your group of stakeholders to agree on a common set of character and

Eiane Parke, **Mass Appeal**, *NASP Magazine*, November 2000
Full PDF available at www.12habits4allofus.org

Excerpt from: **The Caring Habit of the Month Story**
One promising response to the Littleton tragedy

OCTOBER 2000

The Caring Habit of the Month Story – One promising response to the Littleton tragedy.

by Elaine Parke, MBA, CS, CM, NSA*
*Dedicated to children and youth, everywhere.

The volcanics that erupted in Littleton, Colorado in 1999, had been growing in American Schools since the late 1940s. Back then the problems were talking, gum chewing and noise. Today we fear guns, drugs and violence. Youth "well-being" is challenged in ways we've never faced before.

This is a story about a promising strategy, the Caring Habit of the Month Adventure. This strategy is based on Travis Hirschi's theory that "deviant behavior is reduced when societal bonding is improved." It is demonstrating it can support efforts to reduce youth violence by cohesively nourishing the caring fabric of our schools, our families, and our communities. How can it help? By intentionally integrating tools we've never had available before -- the principles that drive 20th century media.

TODAY, with the generous support of Highmark Blue Cross Blue Shield and CBS-KDKA-TV 2, a two-year "Caring Habit of the Month Adventure" curriculum project is underway at Aliquippa Middle School near Pittsburgh. This school serves a challenged community, one of six districts on the Pennsylvania Governor's "Watch List." CBS-KDKA-TV 2 has devoted one million dollars per year of public service air time to this campaign. Artwork and printing for "turn-key" caring habits programming for middle schools is already available.

The Caring Habit strategy combines "in-school" media elements with the community, the home and the classroom to inspire "connectedness" and mutual caring amongst youth and adults. It is truly "a whole community raising each child" by improving our own caring behaviors towards youth, and between one another. Its twelve themes advocate the GOLDEN RULE of mutual respect.

It all began as the outgrowth of my own frustrations as a concerned mother and a gang-intervention/youth volunteer. Teachers and professionals who want to make a difference know that our time and resources are never enough to meet the needs of youth. Meanwhile, in my professional life as a corporate marketing executive, I went to my office each day, and use media principles to routinely educate and influence the behavior and buying attitudes of hundreds of thousands of people.

One fall day, in 1987 the light bulb went off. I realized that a plan to combine proven media principles with healthy educational and civic responsibility objectives could help keep our efforts to meet youth needs -- from failing. The plan was to "organize" a systematic year-round campaign of simple actionable monthly themes about caring behaviors and attitudes. It is significant that a month is about the length of time that researchers say it takes to make a habit out of consistently repeated actions.

My assumptions about the importance of "caring" as the focus of a youth solution were confirmed by the SEARCH Institute of Minneapolis, MN. Their 1997 study of 90,000 American youth confirmed Hirschi's "societal bonding" theory. The study concluded:

"Belief in the fact that they are loved, valued, and cared for by their parents, at school and in the community is the most powerful predictor of the health and well-being* of youth today."

*The report defines well-being as a heightened resistance to all negative influences; violence, school failure, drugs, crime, sex, etc.

With Caring Habits as a year-round time-based focusing system, we can converge the power of media on the principles of caring relationships without competing against ourselves for print and air time. Media experts know it takes six (6) imprints of a single message to imbed a thought or idea into long term memory. Media experts apply the same repetition, reminding and reinforcement techniques that educators use to teach the alphabet or the multiplication tables -- but they can electronically multiply their messages to teach millions.

These media principles and others -- are why advertising works -- and why the negative content of media has been a powerful influence on youth. Advertisers also use BRAND names like "McDonald's" to help people remember their products, like hamburgers. In designing the Caring Habit strategy, I considered that collectively, we know twelve potential BRAND names. They are the names of the months of the year. These months each provide a 30-day period of time for intensive messaging of a theme - the approximate length of time it takes to instill a habit.

Advertisers also use colors as cues to remind people of their products. The Caring Habit plan gives each month a caring habit and a color that means something related to each habit. For instance, the September caring habit is "Do Your Best," and the color is AWARD Gold. It is planned that the name of each month and its color, will become recognized as a "brand name" for one specific caring behavior theme?

Eiane Parke, **The Caring Habit of the Month Story**, *NASP Magazine*, October 2000

Download a printable PDF of the full text of this article at: www.12habits4allofus.org

Using Media to Inspire Unity and Citzenship

Eiane Parke, **Using Media to Inspire Unity and Citzenship**,
Principal Leadership, April 2005
Full PDF available at www.12habits4allofus.org

Statistical Summary of 12 Unity Habts
produced for the release of *Becoming Unity*

Statistical Summary of Documented Results of 12 Unity Habits System
(formerly known as 12 Caring Habits)

Measured School Survey Results:
(2000-2003) 14,000 students, (35 schools and 27 after-schools)

Dr. Edmund M. Ricci, PhD, - Dept. Chairman, University of Pittsburgh Graduate School of Public Health...

"The number of honor roll students appears to be increasing in the Caring Habit schools while indicators of disciplinary actions are declining."

18.5% increase in school honor rolls
22.5% decrease in student detentions
85% reported more caring respectful behaviors
62.5% reported working harder in school
51% reported completing homework more often
54.5% have learned to set positive goals and achieve them
61% have done "something nice for someone at home or at school

Highmark Blue Cross Blue Shield – Intensive Pilot School Results (1998-2000)

• Pennsylvania State Standard School Performance (PSSA)
• Science scores increased one year and nine months
• Math scores increased one year and six months
• Student honor rolls increased 39%

Several Representative Random Student Survey Comments

"I am now nice to the people I used to be mean to. This is COOL. I might even get better grades."

"Kids do much better and keeps their minds off trouble."

"It's trying to tell us not to do stuff before we do it."

"Gets bad people and turn them into good people like the rest of the school."

"I don't have such an attitude anymore with anyone unless they make me angry."

"I act nicer, resolve conflicts in having a bad attitude with everybody, even teachers."

"These are good habits to change your bad ones."

Measured Community Survey Results:

• Specific **improved behavior reported by 39%** of the (aware) community citizens out of 30,000

• Contributed to a **10% decline in the number of criminal case dockets** after a 12-year period of rising court statistics.

• Resulted in a **72% reported improvement in positive community connectedness and improved climate.**

Several Representative Random Community Resident Survey Comments

"Very worthwhile - brings parents, children and others together into better relationships."

"A community-based program designed to improve morale of community and to bring people together. Gets away from stressing the bad things all the time."

"A group of people who have gotten together to encourage community togetherness."

Download a printable PDF of this document at:
www.12habits4allofus.org

ACKNOWLEDGMENTS

Cover Design
Kurt Griffith, Berkeley Springs, WV

Page Layout, Graphic & Type Design, and Typography
Kurt Griffith, Fantastic Realities Studio
Berkeley Springs, WV

Quotation Research
Kaaren Radecki, Pittsburgh, PA

Author Photographer
Stephen Fischer, Elbert CO

Additional Photography
Elaine Parke

Fortune Cookie Philosophies
Ty Ling Fortune Cookie Company

Front Cover Quotation
With permission from Tim Schriver

Back Cover Quotation
With permission from Melvin H. Steals PhD.

Interior Quotations
Multi-sourced on internet and credited - from many great hearts around the world, old and young, past and present.